Postcards

from the

Sky

Spread your wings!

Erin S

Spread your wings!

Erin

Postcards from the Sky

Adventures of an Aviatrix

by

Erin Seidemann

SHE WRITES PRESS

Published 2015
Printed in the United States of America
ISBN: 978-1-63152-826-2
Library of Congress Control Number: 2015942932

Book design by Stacey Aaronson

For information, address:
She Writes Press
1563 Solano Ave #546
Berkeley, CA 94707

She Writes Press is a division of SparkPoint Studio, LLC.

Names and identifying characteristics have been changed to protect the privacy of certain individuals.

To my parents
For always believing in me and encouraging me no matter what I did
and even if you wished I hadn't

Introduction |

"I am not the same having seen the moon shine
on the other side of the world."
—MARY ANNE RADMACHER HERSHEY

I AM AN UNLIKELY TRAVELER. I'VE BLOWN CHUNKS, puked, hurled, whatever you want to call it, in places all over the world. All too easily, I get carsick, airsick, seasick, and every other kind of sick there is. I also don't like sitting in one place for very long, and there's a mind-boggling amount of sitting involved in traveling—an act that seems contradictory to travel itself since travel is *supposed* to be about moving. Furthermore, I am a germophobe, a neat freak, and an obsessive-compulsive—all things that make me cringe at the idea of being stuck in a crowded airplane, bus, train, or boat.

All of which is to say: I should hate traveling. And yet there is something about it—something about seeing the world from a different perspective, the endless variety it has to offer—that keeps me crawling (often literally, given all my extra-special bouts of traveling sickness) back for more.

Case in point: While on a family vacation to Italy one year when I was a teenager, some unknown malady made me delirious to the point of hallucinating, and I apparently tried, in my raving state, to commit suicide in my sleep. Screaming "Dad ran over my foot!" I ran to the open floor-to-ceiling window and attempted to leap out of our eighth-story hotel room. When my mother grabbed me by the waist of my pants—just in time, my family tells me—I woke with a jolt to find myself teetering at the edge of the opening, one foot planted on the floor, the other dangling in midair. But even as I hung there, one step shy of certain death, my first thought wasn't, "What the hell just happened?" No, as I looked down at the landscape before me, the faint sound of a woman singing opera carrying to me on the breeze, my first thought was, "Damn, this place is beautiful!"

And that's how it's always been for me. Even with travel's many drawbacks—insomnia-inducing time differences, bottled-water-only-even-to-brush-your-teeth-or-you'll-be-sorry locales, spirit-crushing airline delays, and even once having my hard suitcase sliced open by God knows what and then placed on the turnstile as if nothing had happened, my unmentionables spewing out of the jagged edge—I just can't get enough of it.

Given everything I've just told you, it's even harder to explain how, or why, an unlikely traveler like me eventually became a still-more-unlikely pilot. After her first airplane ride, Amelia Earhart said, "As soon as we left the ground, I knew I had to fly." I *wish* I'd had that kind of conviction. Far from it. As a kid, I always got airsick on even the most docile airliner, arriving at my destination sweaty, clammy, pale, dizzy, and lethargic. Who could have guessed that the teenager whose face went white and stomach went green every time she went airborne would go on to want to attempt flying herself—and then fall head over heels in love with it?

You might think that my hatred of commercial airline flights was what motivated me to take flying lessons, but it wasn't. I still have to take them for long trips, and while my disdain for them only grows as time goes on and fares go up, delays become more frequent, and security searches become more personal, I don't think that alone could have gotten me in the pilot's seat. It wasn't hatred but love—love for seeing new things and meeting new people, by whatever means of transportation—that pushed me to become a pilot.

I TOOK MY FIRST SMALL AIRPLANE RIDE WHEN I WAS seventeen and had just graduated from high school. It was a seaplane outing from Key West to the Dry Tortugas that took us over half a dozen shipwrecks in crystal-clear water. It was an amazing sight that would not have been visible from any other mode of transport. And the little plane brought us, in just a few minutes, to an island that seemed to me like another world—an uninhabited idyll where we snorkeled in pool-colored water full of huge turtles and barracudas (the sight of which prompted screams from my mother to swim back to land), and I floated motionless, in awe of the beauty surrounding me. There was also something I noticed when the seaplane pilot came back to pick us up: he had tan lines on his feet from wearing flip-flops. At the sight of them, I wondered if I could become a seaplane pilot so I could have a job that allowed me to get tan lines like his.

When we landed back in Key West, my parents made a big deal about how, when we were coming in to land at the island, the pilot had been forced to perform a "go around" when a boat crossed his path just before we were to touch down. I was completely oblivious to that near-miss, as I had my face plastered to the plane's side window, making a greasy nose print on the glass, spellbound and wide-eyed by the view outside. All I knew was that I was sad the trip was over.

This small airplane flight showed me that even in a

relatively slow aircraft with limited fuel capacity, you can discover a new world, meet its strange inhabitants, and still be back home in time for dinner. Since becoming a pilot, I've found that flying has not only given me more opportunities to travel but also new experiences in the course of the journey itself. The old saying that the adventure is in the journey must have originated with small airplane pilots, because I've found that my voyages to and from a planned destination are often more adventurous and more memorable than the things I do once I get there, *if* I get there.

And sometimes, solely by virtue of having flown alone to a faraway place in a small plane, things happen differently than if I had arrived there with the masses in an airliner or on a cruise ship. When people hear that I flew my own plane in, they want to know more about me and why I chose to fly there by myself. And because of the extended conversations that ensue, I also learn more about them. Each encounter is more personal than if I had been sitting like a drone on a flight with three hundred other strangers traveling anonymously.

It is for all these reasons and countless more that this unlikely and occasionally still-queasy traveler decided to become a pilot. Through hurricanes, blizzards, volcanic ash clouds, earthquakes, floods, and every other catastrophe Mother Nature can dish out—with the exception, so far, of a tsunami—I have trudged on, hungry for that next adventure, for that experience that is anything but funny at the time, but which makes for extremely funny retelling once I'm safely home. I've had enough adventures born solely of surrendering to the wind to believe that a certain loss of control makes a trip that much more interesting. As Jimmy Dean, a member of the Merchant Marines and Air Force who later came to fame as a country singer, once said: "I can't change the wind, but I can adjust my sails."

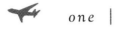 *one* | INSTILLING WANDERLUST

And that's the wonderful thing about family travel:
it provides you with experiences that will remain locked forever
in the scar tissue of your mind.

—DAVE BARRY

$\mathcal{M}$Y EARLIEST TRAVEL MEMORY IS OF A FAMILY vacation we took to Washington, DC when I was five years old and my brother was ten. Our very basic van (this was in 1985, before minivans became ubiquitous) was broken into one night, and the thief stole a neat space shuttle mobile that my parents had bought for me at the Air and Space Museum. I cried hysterically over the loss. I *really* liked that mobile. What kid doesn't dream of being an astronaut? Never mind that the thief also stole more important stuff, like my brother's clarinet. He couldn't play it worth a damn anyway.

I don't remember anything else from that trip except that it was miserably cold. Nothing happy. Nothing enjoyable. Just unbearable cold and the petty thievery of something I had grown very attached to over the space of the few hours it was in my possession. Not exactly a warm and fuzzy welcome to traveling.

We took vacations in that van at least once a year. My parents were still struggling after a business failure, but they knew that we would all be better off for having traveled, even if only domestically. My mom always brought garbage bags for us to pee in so we wouldn't have to stop. After we used them, she tied them off and put them on the floorboard next to the door so none of us would accidentally step on them. She is always thinking ahead, my mom.

When I was a little older, my parents upgraded to a bigger van, one of those dreamy ones (for a kid, at least) with a five-inch TV facing the back seats. (This was *major* technology in its day, a piece of equipment so completely misunderstood that the first question most people would ask was "Does it have cable?") My dad wired a VCR to it so we could watch our favorite movies while traveling. My brother and I got to take turns picking movies, and I—revealing my obsessive-compulsive tendencies early on—always chose the same one: *Alice in Wonderland*. To this day, my family still changes the channel when it comes on, having memorized it for life years ago.

I liked to sit upside down in the van's big, cushy chairs, my legs pointing up the back, and imagine that I was a space shuttle pilot. My stomach didn't like that much, but my imagination sure did. The van's turns, stops, and accelerations became pulling Gs on liftoff or spinning out of control after being shot by aliens. The van also had a small, round table, which could be plugged into one of two metal holes in the floor, that my brother and I used for space-flight planning and debriefing—as long as *Alice in Wonderland* wasn't playing, that is.

Unfortunately, it was also on those early family trips that my brother and I developed a rather unpleasant tradition: one of us always got sick. Very sick. Guaranteed. And we took turns with it—so reliably, in fact, that when my brother was puking his guts up into the hotel room ice bucket in Jackson Hole, Wyoming while I was hungrily asking my mom for some chicken fingers, we all knew that whatever trip we took next, I'd be the one in misery. In Santa Fe, New Mexico, I had the pleasure of throwing up into a cafeteria tray, the closest thing my father could grab when I uttered the dreaded and weakly spoken words, "Dad, I think I'm gonna—"

You would think all that nausea would have dampened my enthusiasm for travel, but it didn't. I loved our family trips. There was such variety in the scenery, the people, the language, and the lifestyles we encountered during our travels—even just within the United States, where you can have lush greenery in the South and Midwest, a flat, brick-red sandscape in the West that looks like the surface of Mars, and a frozen white winter wonderland in the North. At an early age, it became clear to me that traveling would have to be a huge part of my life. Nothing was going to keep me from seeing the things I wanted to see— especially not a little bit of regurgitated food.

BY THE TIME I WAS IN MY TEENS, MY PARENTS HAD STARTED another business, this one successful. They were now able to save up enough money each year so that our family trips were to Europe with airsickness bags rather than to Florida with pee bags.

It was during those international trips that I began to realize how special traveling is. Traveling in the borders of my own country had expanded my world, but visiting other countries blew it wide open. I loved observing all the odd (to me) things that people from other cultures did—some of them individual quirks, others local traditions. On a trip to Italy, in a small town, the drivers all had their windows down and were banging angrily on their car doors, all of which were dented from the abuse. It took us hours to figure out that horns were not allowed there and that the banging was their improvised substitution for a horn. In Norway, we reluctantly ate salmon pizza, bewildered by the fact that we were seemingly the only ones there who thought no fish of any kind should ever be used as a pizza topping. And at Ashbury, an ancient stone altar in England similar to Stonehenge, we witnessed a woman bear-hugging ... a rock. Though I walked through most of Europe with my headphones on—the better to ignore my parents—I was paying attention, and my highly impressionable teenage mind was abuzz with the things I was seeing and learning.

The world was showing me that traveling came with incredible experiences that could not be ignored, and the lesson stuck—as did the memories. I can't tell you what I had for lunch yesterday, but if you ask me to tell you about a trip I took twenty years ago, I can go on and on.

WHEN I WAS THIRTEEN, A FAMILY TRIP TO SCOTLAND inspired me to start taking bagpipe lessons. I started them as soon as we got home to New Orleans, and within the year I was playing professionally at O'Flaherty's Irish Channel Pub in the French Quarter alongside my bagpipe teacher. A year later he moved away, and I kept playing there, now as a fourteen-year-old soloist.

Bagpipes, as you may know, are not exactly a commonly played instrument. So when Patrick Taylor, a very wealthy oil magnate who occasionally came by the pub, wanted a bagpipe player for his mother's funeral, I got the call. I was twenty years old, and had personally benefited from a program Taylor had set up—Taylor Opportunity Program for Students, or TOPS, which allowed Louisiana students with good enough grades to attend a state college completely free. I thought the world of the man. So when my boss from the pub called and said Patrick Taylor wanted me to play for him, I jumped, flattered that he enjoyed my music.

The funeral was to be held at Taylor's ranch in Mississippi, and he sent a private plane to collect me, two other musicians from the pub, and the Irish ambassador (oil magnates apparently have friends in high places) one evening. The pilot let me sit up front with him while the other guys got drunk in back, and I couldn't get over the beauty of flying in darkness. Sure, I had flown at night before in airliners, up at thirty-some-thousand feet, where all you can see is blackness—maybe a few stars, if it's a particularly clear night. But this was different. We were much closer to the Earth, and I could see the glowing outlines of the small towns we passed, each with its own distinct shape, enveloped on every side by astounding darkness. I felt like an astronaut in the black vacuum of space, trying to find my way in an endless sea of nothingness. And it didn't hurt that I wasn't feeling the slightest bit nauseous, even with all the vertigo-inducing voids between cities where there was nothing to tell my brain what was up and what was down. The night was still and the ride was smooth, and I didn't feel even a twinge of that queasiness that usually hit me when I was up in the air.

I wondered how the pilot could fly in that black nothingness between cities. I mean, how could he see where he was going? I glanced over at the whirling instruments on the panel in front of him—some moving constantly, some totally still, and all dimly lit in an eerie red glow. I knew they had some meaning to him, but they were completely random puzzles, colors, and shapes to me. How could anyone ever learn to interpret what each of those meant? It looked to me as if they had all gone haywire, as there seemed to be no rhyme or reason to their movements or lack thereof. I also marveled at how uninhabited most of the land was, except for those few small towns dotting the landscape. You hear all the time on the news about the planet being overcrowded, but the view from the air told a vastly different story.

By the time we landed, I had absolutely no idea where we were; the lit rectangle of the runway had appeared seemingly out of nowhere, yet perfectly aligned with the airplane's path. I felt like I had just been the subject of a magic trick: one minute I was back at home at the airport, and the next minute someone had waved a wand and placed our airplane gently down in the one patch of light to be found in all the darkness around us.

Things got much weirder when we landed. Multiple drivers greeted us at the plane and opened the doors to their cars without saying a word. I climbed inside the closest one.

"Where are we going?" I asked, feeling a little uncertain.

The driver glanced at me in the rearview mirror. "Your presence is requested for a welcome drink," he told me. "I'll take you to your room after."

I nodded and settled back in my seat. Minutes later, driving through darkness only slightly illuminated by our dim headlights, we pulled up to a large airplane hangar, and the driver again opened my door for me.

I stepped through the tall hangar doors—and immediately did a double take. There was an animal I didn't quite recognize to my left, frozen in an attack pose, standing almost as high as the ceiling. *What the hell?* I wondered. In another corner stood an extremely large zebra, also frozen. I wondered if the Sprite I'd just been handed had been spiked. I turned slowly around to face the opposite end of the hangar, and there stood a giraffe. My driver, who was standing just inside the door, saw the bewildered look on my face.

"Mr. Taylor killed each of these creatures on safari and had them shipped back here," he explained.

My eyes widened. *Ho-ly COW!*

After I'd finished my soda and shaken a few hands of strangers milling about, my driver motioned for me to follow him. This time a soft-spoken, formal older woman accompanied us. They brought me to one of the many houses used as guest accommodations on the ranch—ours was about the size of the house I grew up in. It was January, and the warmth of the fireplace beckoned, but it was quite late for me, and I was exhausted. I went straight to bed.

The next morning, I woke up, stretched in bed, and walked downstairs to the smell of tea brewing. It was a bright, clear day, so I took a casual peek out the window on the way to the kitchen as I was smoothing my bed-head hair—and almost swallowed my tongue. As far as I could see, there were wild animals everywhere—some very near the house. And these weren't frozen in poses like the ones I'd seen in the hangar the previous night; they were moving and very much alive. I let out a primal squeak of terror and knocked on the window with the back of my hand to make sure it was made of thick glass.

Not wanting to make a fool of myself, I moseyed into the kitchen and tried to act normal, exchanging pleasantries with other guests as I poured myself a cup of tea, my hand still trembling from shock. Then I walked back out of the kitchen so I could check the window again. Was I hallucinating?

One of the other guests followed me. "You just got here last night, right?" she asked.

I nodded.

She opened the front door. "Here," she said nonchalantly, "let me show you around."

I jumped back, but then she stepped out, and, trying to act cool, I reluctantly followed. It was only then that I noticed—to my great relief—that there was a fence between the house and the animals. I sighed audibly and relaxed.

The funeral itself was held that morning in one of the hangars with the big animals. I played "Amazing Grace" and a few other funeral standards, and then I was flown back to New Orleans. By that afternoon, I was back at home, setting my bagpipes down in my room. It was all so surreal. My brain kept begging me to answer the question, *What the hell just happened?* But as disoriented as I felt from the whole experience, I understood one thing: one small airplane had the power to unlock lands and adventures that existed only in my wildest imagination.

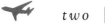 *two* | PREFLIGHT

"*So many men now have lost their lives in airplane accidents that individual addition [sic] to the long list of their names have ceased to cause any really deep emotions except in the minds of their relatives and friends. When a woman is the victim however the feeling of pity and horror is as strong as was that produced by the first of these disasters to men and though there is at present no expectation that aviation should be abandoned by men because of the recognized dangers, the death of Miss Bromwell is almost sure to raise in many minds at least the question if it would not be well to exclude women from a field of activity in which there [sic] presence certainly is unnecessary from any point of view.*"
—THE NEW YORK TIMES EDITORIAL, 1921

EVER SINCE WE'D STARTED DATING, JOHN HAD BEEN talking about taking flying lessons. Becoming a pilot had been a lifelong dream of his, and while it hadn't fit into his old life (he was recently divorced), he was now beginning to feel like it was something he could pursue. Yet he took no steps to actually sign up for lessons. I'm not sure what the hang-up was, but I finally convinced him that he had the two things you need most to fly—time and money—and nothing was holding him back, so he should stop talking about it and start doing it. Actually, I was hoping to buy him his first flying lesson as a birthday present, but my pep talk was apparently a little *too* convincing, because he signed up for a class in San Francisco before I had the chance.

Determined to be a part of this new adventure, I ended up paying for John's *second* lesson—this time in New Orleans, when he came to visit me—and I even went along for the ride. Unfortunately, his instructor insisted on going up and doing "stalls"—a term for stalling the plane's wings so that they no longer produce lift, which makes the plane drop (sometimes sideways) before it can be leveled off again. Stalls are usually quite docile if you enter them in coordinated flight, which involves using the rudders (the foot pedals that control side-to-side movement of the airplane's tail) and ailerons (the "steering wheel" part of the plane that controls turns) in coordination with aerodynamic influences like speed, the propeller slipstream, and crosswinds. But coordinated flight is something that takes practice to do properly, and stalls that occur during *un-*coordinated flight can get a little hairy. Given that this was only John's second lesson, we had a few stall entries that were uncoordinated. When that happens, one wing drops suddenly, and it's damn scary for someone who doesn't know what's going on. I had already started to get a little queasy from the unfamiliar motion of the small airplane, but when the stalls began, I wondered if I would be able to keep my breakfast down.

The instructor finally noticed my discomfort. "If you don't feel well at any point," he said, "you just let me know and we'll go right back to the airport."

"I'd like to go back now," I said weakly. I felt badly that I had to end John's lesson early, but I figured it would end much worse if I ralphed all over the plane.

I'D MET JOHN ABOUT TWO YEARS EARLIER AT HOME IN New Orleans. It was summer, and I had been hired to play bagpipes for a couple's anniversary at their condo in the French Quarter. I had assumed the gig would be held indoors—because who the hell wants to be outside in fancy clothes during a sweltering July day in New Orleans? The condo was lovely and spacious, and when I arrived everyone was inside enjoying hors d'oeuvres and drinks. But since bagpipes are so loud (they have no volume control—the only options are on or off), the couple decided to put me outside on the balcony to play.

The sun was setting, but that didn't alleviate the heat. Bagpipes are a very physically demanding instrument, and my formal kilt and Prince Charlie suit jacket—made of a heavy wool intended for cool Scottish weather—were soaked through with sweat. I thought I might pass out. But every time I stopped to take a short breather and gulp some water to replace the gallons of fluids I was losing in perspiration, the hosts encouraged me to keep playing.

I glanced at my watch and saw that I'd been playing for more than an hour. I knew they soon had dinner reservations for the whole party at the Windsor Court Hotel, just across Canal Street; I figured I was almost finished.

Then the husband came out to the balcony—to pay me and to thank me for coming, I thought.

But no: "We'd like you to play during the ride to the Windsor Court," he said.

Before I could react, he was already ushering me downstairs to the waiting carriages he'd hired to transport the party in style. I started to open my mouth—and he handed over a substantial tip, all in cash. I clamped my mouth shut, smiled, wiped the sweat off my forehead onto my sleeve, and shoved my new wad of cash into my kilt's sporran—what I like to refer to as my "crotch purse"—before climbing into one of the carriages.

I calculated the distance between the couple's condo and the Windsor Court and figured I only had about four or five more minutes of playing to do. I could last that long. Of course, there was also the matter of playing bagpipes in a very jerky carriage traveling down streets littered with potholes. I had been hired to play in some interesting places before: outside a window to wake someone up early in the morning, as a practical joke; at funerals, where my rendition of "Amazing Grace" often brought everyone to tears; and at weddings in which neither party was Scottish, Irish, or any other -ish that would make you think they'd want bagpipes, including one where everyone spoke Spanish and I wondered if I was at the wrong church. But this would be my first time playing in a donkey-drawn carriage.

I'd picked one of the carriages with multiple seating rows so I could wedge myself between two benches in a stance normally reserved for riding a crowded subway. I jammed one foot up against the seat in front of me, shoehorned the other under the seat behind me, and off we went. Just as I was settling into this odd scene, I looked around and realized we were going the wrong way. By the time we'd crisscrossed back down another street, it dawned on me: we were literally turning up and down *every* block in the French Quarter. So much for four or five minutes. Knowing I couldn't make it much longer, I stopped playing for a second to catch my breath.

"Oh, so-and-so lives here, and I told them you were coming," the husband—who, of course, was in the carriage with me—immediately said. "You MUST play." He slipped me some extra money again, so play I did. A short tune. Then I stopped to take another breather. I was getting really dizzy.

"Oh, so-and-so lives on this corner," he egged me on again,

"and I told them you were coming. You simply MUST keep playing!"

This continued every time I stopped, even just for a second, for the next few blocks. Those damned people knew everyone in the entire Quarter, and I felt like the object of their rich people's show-and-tell!

I was a hair's breadth away from passing out when our carriage abruptly pulled over in front of Bacco, an upscale restaurant between Bienville and Conti on Chartres Street.

"Why did we stop?" I asked the lady sitting closest to me between gulps for air.

"We're out of champagne," she informed me gaily.

We simply couldn't have that, now could we?

The anniversary couple and some of the party went inside. The moment they were out of sight, I plopped down on the seat nearest me so hard that the woman sitting on the other end of the row jumped. I gave her a "Don't mind me, I'm just about to pass out" look, which she must have read quite well because she handed me a very welcome cold bottle of water without a word.

The cold water took effect quickly, and just like that I was capable of thinking about something other than dying. My gaze drifted across the street, and I noticed a strikingly handsome man walking by, smoking a cigar. He caught me looking at him and smiled at me. Between my extreme fatigue and lightheadedness and the fact that I had just broken up with my boyfriend a week ago after finding him high on cocaine (an instant deal-breaker for me and something he had sworn was in his past), I wasn't in the best mental state. That's the only explanation I have for why—despite the fact that I'm usually the type that takes months, at minimum, to work up the courage to ask someone out—I suddenly found myself bounding out of the carriage to chase this guy down the street. Funny how a cute guy can make a girl (me, anyway) go from no-way-I-could-lift-a-finger to running down the street in about two seconds flat.

I had no idea what I was going to say to him, but I hoped that something witty, charming, and positively irresistible would come to me before I got there. It didn't.

"What kind of cigar are you smoking?" I asked him, panting from the sudden exertion. This was back when cigars were en vogue, and I had recently dated a Marine whose group of friends had taught me the ins and outs of cigars at one of the Marine Corps Birthday Balls.

Cigar Guy looked puzzled, like he was trying to figure out how and why this person he had just smiled at in passing—as you would a stranger on the bus, not flirtatiously—was now standing in front of him. It took him so long to answer that I thought, *Oh shit. He doesn't speak English. He has no idea what I just said.*

After an uncomfortable eternity, he finally replied, slowly and cautiously, "Uh ... Macanudo."

"Oh yeah, those are okay," I said, wiping my brow with my sleeve again and hoping he couldn't tell that I was practically swimming in my own perspiration. "I much prefer Monte-cristos, though. Have you had one?"

I could hear the anniversary party emerging from Bacco and knew I only had a few seconds, so before he could really answer, I sprang into action: "Can I have your number? I'm almost done with this gig ... maybe we could meet for a drink later?"

He wrote it down with a bemused expression on his face and handed it over.

"Bye!" I said and raced back to the carriage, Cigar Guy's number clenched in my sweaty palm. I jumped back into my spot between rows wearing a totally refreshed look.

"Do you know that man?" the lady who had given me a bottle of water asked, looking perplexed.

"Yep!" I said cheerfully and started playing again, a new-found energy driving my diminished breath onward.

TWO YEARS LATER, "CIGAR GUY"—JOHN—AND I HAD been carrying on a long-distance relationship, with him in San Francisco and me still in New Orleans. He lived in San Francisco but traveled a lot for his work as a sales rep, so we actually got to see each other pretty often, and after quitting what was supposed to be a six-year Ph.D. program after just over a year, I came out to California that summer to spend time with him and contemplate what to do with my life.

While I was there, I started to toy with the idea of moving there permanently. Unfortunately, I had *no idea* what I wanted to do. The Ph.D. program I'd just dropped out of was highly competitive—they only took two new candidates every other year—and I hadn't even considered the possibility that it wouldn't work out. Now that it hadn't, I was aimless and close to broke and knew I had to apply for every job I could find. Over the next couple of months, I applied to more than three hundred jobs in both New Orleans and San Francisco, every-thing from editing to financial planning to grant writing.

Meanwhile, John was hooked on his new hobby. And I appreciated his passion for flying—but I certainly didn't share it. *Why would anyone want to pay a ton of money to go up and get airsick?* I wondered, though I was careful to keep those thoughts to myself.

One day I found John on his stomach on the floor, propped up on his elbows, mumbling incomprehensible calculations, with a bunch of aviation maps, a slide rule (who still uses a slide rule, for chrissakes?), and a lot of pencils spread out all over the floor around him. I took one look at him, at all those books open to instructions on how to do … whatever the hell it was he was doing, and said, "Who would ever want to do something like that *for fun?!* It looks like the world's worst homework assignment!"

Still, I couldn't help but notice that this already overly jolly person was even jollier since he'd started taking flying lessons. What the hell was it about the stuff that was making him so happy? Happier than I had ever seen him? And I had to admit it: his joy was contagious. It made me want to give flying a shot. *Fact of the matter is, I get airsick and that's that,* I told myself. But every time John came home from the airport, he was like a kid on cloud nine. It fast became all he ever talked about, so it was pretty hard for me to not think about it. And when I start to get curious about any topic, the first thing I do is go and buy some books about it. So I went to the transportation section of a local bookstore and bought the book with the catchiest title: *Air Vagabonds.* The picture on the front cover showed a guy hanging on for dear life to an airplane in flight with the door open. *Hmm,* I thought. *Seems interesting enough.*

I started reading right away when I got home that night. And that was when my own addiction began.

The book I bought wasn't just about flying. It was about a type of flying that a very small segment of the flying population actually does: ferry piloting. Ferry pilots are men and women who fly airplanes to a new owner, whether the plane is a new one manufactured in Kansas and bought by someone in Wyoming or an old, unreliable beater sold to a good home ten thousand miles away. These crazy pilots fly across oceans and through storms (not, like commercial airliners, *above* storms, because the ceiling—altitude limit—for those little planes isn't high enough to fly over most bad weather).

These days, when I return from a trip to, say, Europe, I am often asked, "Oh, did you fly your plane there?" Many people don't realize that small planes like my Cessna don't have that kind of range. Even if I fueled up on the East Coast, I'd run out of fuel way less than halfway across the Atlantic. Some of the pilots depicted in *Air Vagabonds* did fly across oceans, but in order to do it they had to outfit their planes with special fuel tanks, often taking out every seat except the pilot's and flying way over the maximum legal weight set by the manufacturer for safety reasons. And even then the airplane often had only enough fuel to make it—on fumes—to Narsarsuaq, Greenland, the popular stopover point for Atlantic transoceanic flights in the days when most airplanes couldn't make it across the pond in a single hop.

The book told story after story of these rare adventures, and just a couple of chapters in, my interest was most definitely piqued: I called the local flight school and scheduled my first flying lesson before even finishing the book. (I also wrote an e-mail to the author, Tony Vallone, telling him I had only started to vaguely consider taking lessons after seeing how happy they were making John but that *Air Vagabonds* had pushed me over the edge to finally do it. We have kept in touch ever since and have shared many a flying story over the years—some of them even true!)

I still wasn't sure I was capable of overcoming my airsickness. But after reading about all those other people's adventures, I was dying to have one of my own. It might be awful. But I at least had to try.

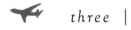 *three* | C L E A R E D   F O R
T A K E O F F

"The world is a book and those who do not travel read only one page."
—ST. AUGUSTINE

I SCHEDULED MY FIRST LESSON IN NEW ORLEANS with Bart, the same instructor who had taken us out for John's second lesson. It was close to Christmastime—a cold, overcast, dreary winter day, not exactly the inviting, clear blue sky that you picture for your first flying lesson. And once we went up, Bart immediately started doing stalls, just like he had when we went up with John.

There are two types of stalls: "power on" stalls, which simulate a stall on departure with full power, and "power off" stalls, which simulate a stall when on approach with little or idle power. The "power on" stall is the more dramatic of the two because you start by climbing at an alarming angle of about 1,000–1,500 feet per minute to dropping at a rate of about 1,000 feet per minute. It's a sudden change of movement that people who get motion sick do not fare well with—and I'm no exception.

As Bart pulled the yoke back to get the nose of the airplane up, I looked straight ahead of me, only sky filled the windshield. It felt completely unnatural.

"Oh my god oh my god oh my god," I blurted on repeat—and then we actually stalled and began our drop, and the pitch of my *oh my god*s got much higher. Somewhere in the back of my mind, I was a little embarrassed by the outburst, having signed up for this torture voluntarily, but I couldn't control it.

After what felt like an eternity, Bart recovered from the stall and got the airplane flying normally again. As we leveled out, I felt the contents of my stomach start to climb too high for comfort. I didn't want to make a big deal of it—I knew I couldn't help my proclivity for airsickness, but I was still embarrassed by it, especially now that I was taking flying lessons—so I just said, "Um ... can we head back? I'm starting to get a little queasy."

When we were back on solid ground and I was starting to feel a little better—still shaky and weak but better—I asked Bart, "Is it normal to get a little motion sick during the first few lessons?"

I was hoping for encouragement. Maybe he would say he used to get a little sick sometimes or that he'd had other students who had and they'd overcome it. But no. All he said was, "You'll get over it."

I wasn't so sure—and I didn't particularly like Bart. But I did like the sensation I'd gotten when the wheels first left the ground and I realized I was flying—really flying!: the view of my city from the little plane, and the satisfaction of putting the contraption back on the ground, right where we'd found it, at the end of the lesson. And if this was how I felt after seeing just a small sliver of the earth from a plane, what would it be like if I could do this all the time—if I could explore the United States and beyond from that vantage point?

For the first few nights after that first lesson, I couldn't sleep; I kept coming up with more and more possibilities, obsessed with imagining what other places would look like from the air. One short lesson, and my brain was already working overtime.

THE MORE I BEGAN TO CONSIDER FLYING AS A SERIOUS pursuit, the more I took it upon myself to learn about the field of aviation. What I discovered was that many places in the United States and around the world are inaccessible by commercial aircraft. According to the 2011–2015 National Plan of Integrated Airport Systems (NPIAS), published by the U.S. Department of Transportation and the Federal Aviation Administration (FAA), of 5,170 airports open to the public, only 503 offer commercial service. The 4,667 public airports that don't are small ones that many people don't know about but that are easily accessible to small aircraft. These small aircraft come under the heading of "general aviation."

I dug a little deeper and learned that general aviation is a ridiculously broad term that encompasses a vast number of very different types of flying: recreational flights, emergency transport of patients and organs, agriculture-related flights (such as the work performed by crop dusters and forest rangers), police and traffic watch, border patrol, charter flights, sightseeing flights, photo flights, skydiving flights, flight training, disaster relief, and pretty much any other kind of non-military flying that is not scheduled commercial service. General aviation also provides more than 1 percent of the U.S. gross domestic product.

All this information was really starting to add up in my head. I'm not the kind of person who likes touristy places. So what better way to reach those off-the-beaten-path locales than by small plane? I kept taking lessons and got in a total of six in

New Orleans with Bart (or Fart, as the mechanic at the flight school referred to him) before finally landing a job as an editor at a small financial services company in San Francisco. I had been looking for a job specifically in San Francisco for months, ever since John's request for a transfer to Houston had been turned down and we'd realized that I was the more portable of the two of us. So, when I got the job, I said goodbye to Fart and headed west.

There are so many things that can get in the way of pursuing a dream—but when it's something you really want, those things become small speed bumps. Bart and his nausea-inducing stalls were one such speed bump, but (fortunately both for my flying future and my equilibrium) getting that job in San Francisco allowed me to sail right over it. I had happily figured out in my six short lessons with Bart that, like most cases of motion sickness, as long as I was flying and not just riding along while he did the flying, I usually felt fine (except for days when we worked on maneuvers with lots of turns). In the years to come, I would face far worse obstacles—even some that felt more like walls than bumps.

 *four* | A LITTLE
TURBULENCE

"San Francisco is 49 square miles surrounded by reality."
—PAUL KANTNER

"San Francisco is like a box of cereal.
Get rid of the nuts and fruits and you still have the flakes!"
—JAY LENO

I HAD A GRAND TOTAL OF ABOUT $6,000 WHEN I left New Orleans. Once I had used it to pay the movers and cover my first and last months' rent on my new apartment in San Francisco, I was left with ... well ... nothing. I had originally assumed that I'd move in with John, what with rent prices being what they are in the Bay Area and my just having started my first full-time job, but—to my surprise and secret disappointment—a few weeks before my move, he informed me that he had been looking for a separate place for me. I comforted myself with the thought that, since he was fifteen years older and, theoretically, wiser, he probably had good reason for deciding that it would be better for us to live in separate apartments. My parents definitely wouldn't have gone for us living together, anyway—so rather than ask him why he didn't want to cohabit, I decided to just go with it.

But about two months later, after two years of maintaining a mostly successful long-distance relationship, John and I broke up. I suppose some things work well on the road but not necessarily in daily life. And we were both changing: I was encountering the reality of life outside of academia for the first time, and he was still adapting to his new, post-divorce life. We didn't have any major problems or blowups; we just sort of fell apart.

The problem was, besides my coworkers, I knew absolutely no one else in San Francisco. And even though I had visited San Francisco a few times before my big move, the culture shock I was experiencing was huge. For one thing, the apartment John had found for me was what he'd called "the nicest thing you'll find around here for this price," but to me it was a complete dump. A really damned expensive dump. It was a tiny studio apartment on the fifth floor of an ugly Victorian building with a urine-scented lobby, located on Stockton Street in downtown San Francisco, about a block from Chinatown. The closet in my apartment was so small that I had to hang my clothes at a 45-degree angle so I could still close the sliding-mirror door. I'd told John I wanted to be able to walk to work when I first moved there, and apparently this was the only thing around that fit that description and my price range.

The move itself was one that could have headlined the evening news, and, since my TV wasn't hooked up yet, I'm not sure it didn't. Think of the population of a big city like San Francisco, where almost no one who lives there is actually from there, and think of how many times a moving van must drive through its streets every day. Millions of moving vans have moved people to San Francisco with no problem. But not mine. Mine bottomed out on the crest of one of San Francisco's famously steep hills about a block from my apartment. Unfortunately, it did so on one of the metal channels in the middle of the cable car rails where the actual cable runs underground. So there I was—standing in the middle of a major thoroughfare in bustling San Francisco, freezing my ass off in the thick, unfamiliar spring fog, my moving van stuck on the hill, the police and the San Francisco Municipal Transportation Agency trying to close the street and re-route traffic around it, and everyone pissed off at me like it was my fault. I have no idea how they finally got the truck unstuck, because by that time I had already fled inside my apartment to hide from the drama and curl up in a fetal position on the bare floor—the only thing in there since everything I owned was still on that truck. At that moment, I felt like more of an outsider than I ever had—including in countries where I didn't even speak the language.

If only the apartment had sucked, and everything else had been great, I could have dealt with the cramped space and smelly lobby. But everything else wasn't great. The area I was living in was a concrete jungle; I saw only a few small trees on my walk to work, and those were struggling to stay alive under the constant overcast of cold fog. The traffic was horrendous. The noise was dizzying. And common courtesy simply didn't seem to exist. People didn't even give up their seats on BART for pregnant women and elderly people. With every negative encounter, my transition to life in the Bay Area became just that much more strained.

The one saving grace of San Francisco was that, soon after I was settled in my thimble-sized apartment, I started taking flying lessons again. Even though John and I had broken up, we still talked, and he set me up with his instructor, Bill.

"He's a good pilot," John told me. "He can teach you a lot. But just so you know, he's late—honestly, the man's so flaky he would lose his head if it weren't screwed on. But when it comes to planes, he *really* knows what he's doing."

John had mentioned that besides being a flight instructor, Bill was also a commercial pilot for one of the major US carriers; I wondered how he could be that flaky and keep his job. I figured the description was just typical John: he tended to expect too much from others. I blew it off and scheduled my first lesson with Bill.

THE FLYING CLUB WHERE BILL TAUGHT WAS THE LARGEST of its kind in the country, with about sixty airplanes of all different types available for rent. I liked that it was a club rather than a school: a club is often owned by its members and tends to be a place for pilots of all levels to come and hang out.

I arrived at the appointed time and sat on the couch inside the flying club. I waited ... and waited ... and waited for Bill. After about twenty minutes, in walked a guy with a severe limp, unruly hair, and a half-untucked shirt. Even in all his unkempt-ness, he was actually kind of cute, in a homeless puppy sort of way, anyway.

I had decided the newcomer was just one of the students there, but then he walked up to me, stuck out his hand, and said, "Erin?"

So this was Bill.

Before we got into the airplane, Bill sat down on the couch with me and looked through my logbook—only six entries detailing my short flights with Bart.

"So," he said, handing back the logbook. "What are your goals in aviation?"

Goals? Hmm. I hadn't even thought of that. I shrugged. "I just want to take flying lessons."

"Well, do you want be an airline pilot?" he asked, cocking

his head slightly to the side. "Or just stick to smaller airplanes?"

He really was good-looking. *That's not why you're here,* I reminded myself, and tried to focus on the question at hand. But the truth was, I didn't know. This was all so new to me; I wasn't even sure what my options were. "Well ..." I said slowly, "let's see how this goes first—see if I like it or not—and then can I go from there? Or do I need to know now?"

"It helps to know your goals so we can tailor your training to where you want to go with it," Bill said.

"All I know is that I like the idea of flying and where it can take me," I said. "I wasn't crazy about my instructor back home"—I was intentionally avoiding any mention of my tendency to get motion sick at this point; he didn't need to know that yet—"and John highly recommended you, so I just want to see how it goes."

"How is John, by the way?" Bill asked. "I haven't seen him in a while."

Cute guy asking about ex-boyfriend? Awkward!

"He's fine, as far as I know," I said, consciously trying to put some distance between John and me in Bill's mind. "He moved up to Mill Valley, so he's taking lessons at some airport up there now since it's closer."

Bill nodded. "Makes sense." He stood and squinted down at me. "Well, let's go flying!"

I jumped up from the couch, my logbook clenched in my hand, and we walked out to the flight line. On the way, I asked as politely as I could about his limp, figuring maybe he'd been in an accident when flying in a war and maybe it'd be a story he told proudly.

He winced a little at the question. "I've had a bad hip since birth," he explained, "and it's getting worse."

He had a helpless tone in his voice as he said it, and I was immediately sorry I had asked. But also a little bit endeared to him. He really was like a homeless puppy; it made me want to take care of him. Once we turned our attention back to flying, however, Bill was nothing but professional and competent. He explained things very clearly, in a way I could understand, and once we were up in the air, it immediately became apparent that he had an uncanny ability to make the airplane do exactly what he wanted it to do. His experience as a lifelong career pilot showed in his flying skills; it was like he was one with the plane.

His people skills, on the other hand, needed some serious work—something that became clear as we were flying over the East Bay when he got on the radio with NorCal (short for Northern California) Approach, the radar facility that handles all the Bay Area traffic. I listened as a woman pilot came over the frequency to announce her arrival in the airspace on her way to land at San Francisco International Airport (SFO). She made the standard radio call in a very professional manner and ended it by stating her airline, flight number, and the word "heavy," indicating that her plane is certified for a takeoff weight of 255,000 pounds or more. We are talking a big-ass plane—probably a 767, 777, 747, A330, or A340. Any pilot who can handle a plane like that demands respect. Unless, of course, you're Bill.

"Well," he said, "there goes another empty kitchen!"

I wondered how that comment was linked in any way to what the pilot had just said. I didn't get it—or at least thought it couldn't possibly mean what I thought it did. "Is that a pilot expression?" I asked. "What does it mean?"

"Oh, that's what male pilots say to each other in the cockpit when a chick pilot comes on the radio," Bill said jovially. "You know—it means there's another woman in the cockpit who should really be back in the kitchen, where she belongs."

My jaw dropped. *What an asshole!* Here I was, a woman, paying him sixty dollars an hour for flying lessons, and he was saying something this atrociously chauvinistic *to my face?* What the hell was wrong with this guy?!

Later, Bill would tell me another old "joke" that begins, "Why do women make such bad pilots?" (Because the general public often judges a pilot based mostly on his or her landing, being able to estimate the plane's distance above the ground in a landing flare using your peripheral vision is an important skill.) The answer—delivered as the joke teller stretches his fingers two or three inches apart—is, "They can't judge distance in the landing flare very well because they've always been told that *this* is six inches."

By the time he told me that zinger, I knew him well enough not to be surprised by it. For now, though—still in the middle of my first lesson with him—that one "empty kitchen" comment was more than enough to piss me off. Bill had seemed perfectly affable on the ground; now I was convinced he needed a formal course in sensitivity training, perhaps accompanied by some behavioral therapy. I didn't say another word for the rest of the flight besides the minimum of what was required to get us back to the airport.

I should have landed the plane and walked away—run away—after that first lesson. But despite how infuriated I was by Bill's sexist comment, I found him attractive, and I was also impressed by his skills as a pilot. I wanted to keep him as my instructor. So—against my better judgment—I did.

As is probably apparent by now, I was entering only lightly charted territory as I began my training to become a female pilot. The world of aviation, as Bill's comments and stories make abundantly clear, is largely male. As of 2013, the FAA shows there were 599,086 licensed pilots in the United States—and of those, only 39,621 were women (that's 6.6 percent). If you exclude student pilot certificates from that count—and it makes sense to do so, since many student pilots never actually finish the training to get the basic pilot certificate and become a private pilot—the actual figures diminish to 478,801 total licensed pilots, only 25,216 of which are women (this works out to an even smaller 5.3 percent). And the female-to-male pilot ratio *outside* the US is probably even more dramatic.

The number of women pilots is growing, but it's happening very slowly—and no wonder, with misogynistic guys like Bill serving as their instructors. And unfortunately, Bill is not the only male pilot I've met who's like that. Not even close. I continue to encounter unbelievably shortsighted statements like "There goes another empty kitchen" when I'm hanging out with other pilots. Another favorite is the more straightforward "Girls can't fly." But from that first lesson with Bill, I was determined to prove that indeed we can fly—and we can do it well.

five

AVIATE,
NAVIGATE,
COPULATE

*"A male pilot is a confused soul who talks about women when flying
and about flying when with women."*
—ANONYMOUS

OU'D THINK I WOULD HAVE LEARNED MY LESSON about Bill's character based on his comments in the plane. But no. I often have a hard head. The hardest. No, even harder than that. Not only did I not tell him where he could stick his chauvinism and dump him on the spot as my instructor, I actually started *dating* him.

I will admit that dating the teacher—in this case, the flight instructor—had its perks. A typical date with Bill involved flying someplace exciting for a date, parking in a secluded spot at the airport, having sex in the plane, and then heading out to go exploring. We even had our "own" parking spot at Half Moon Bay airport, far away from the runway, where we had unobstructed views of the beautifully picturesque Pacific coast landscape and guaranteed privacy. It afforded all the great atmosphere of outdoor sex without the downside of getting dirt, sand, or grass in our clothes and crevices. This ritual became a regular part of our dating life, and it only deepened my obsession with my new hobby. Sex was one of my favorite activities, and now I could combine it with my recent great passion: flying. I was more than willing to look past whatever faults Bill might have in order to keep this incredible new lifestyle alive. (There may also have been the occasional fooling around while in the air, but I'm not at liberty to go into details if I'd like to keep my license with the FAA!)

With all the sex we were having, I may have sometimes lost sight of the fact that the real reason for these "lessons" was to learn how to fly—but despite that, I was still picking up the basics of flying, including the Holy Trinity of aviation emergency tasks: aviate, navigate, and communicate. These procedures are always listed in order of their importance during any emergency, starting with aviate. In the case of engine failure, for example, the most critical thing to do is to keep flying the airplane; you don't want to spend so much energy concentrating on the other two tasks that you do something stupid. Some pilots have ended up crashing a plane while trying to fiddle with whatever was causing the problem, even when it was something that wouldn't have made the airplane fall out of the sky (like a radio problem, for instance). So the rule is, aviate first, and then—if and only if you have the time and resources to do so—you can worry about navigating, and after that communicating with air traffic control. You will hear pilots say "aviate, navigate, communicate" about everything. It's our mantra. I figured Bill and I were inventing our own version of that rhyme: aviate, navigate, copulate.

DURING TRAINING AS A STUDENT PILOT, YOUR FIRST major milestone is your first "solo" because it means you're ready to fly without the safety net of having an instructor sitting next to you. After about twenty lessons—many of which were cut short by my ongoing bouts of airsickness—I was past ready to solo, but the weather had not been cooperating. So when one of those famous, clear California days finally arrived, I could barely contain my excitement. I was going to do it. I was going to fly a plane *all by myself.*

Bill and I had planned for this moment, and we'd decided that when the weather finally turned, we'd fly together until we found an airport that had a light wind heading straight down the runway. (First solos are not allowed when there's a strong crosswind on the runway; crosswind landing is a skill, and it's not one that a rookie pilot like me has developed in time for their first solo.) So we jumped in a plane and went airport-hopping all over the northern Bay Area trying to find the perfect conditions, until finally we heard a report that the airstrip in Petaluma, up in wine country, had what we were looking for.

By the time we landed in Petaluma, I was raring to fly solo.

"Go ahead and taxi to the ramp," Bill said. "I'll get out there."

When we got to the ramp, however, he flashed me a grin. "But before you solo," he said, and he grabbed my hand and put it directly on his hard dick.

I rolled my eyes. This was normally a request I was more than happy to oblige—but today, "copulate" was not the item on our Holy Trinity list that I was interested in doing! Still, I didn't want to put him in a bad mood, so I sighed and surrendered to the moment.

On the plus side, he didn't really care whether I had an

orgasm or not (typical Bill, as I was learning the hard way—no pun intended), so our tryst was at least quick. When we were done, I shooed him out the door. I was so excited about soloing that I didn't even bother to put my pants back on after he climbed out of the plane.

Just before closing the passenger door, Bill called into the plane, "Whatever you do, don't turn the radio on!" He knew that I liked to listen to local AM radio stations through the ADF (Automatic Direction Finder, a now-outdated navigational instrument that picks up AM radio frequencies) whenever we were flying in range of the signal, but today he wanted me to concentrate on flying the plane without him.

I ignored him completely, of course: as soon as he was gone, I jammed in the button that switched on the ADF sound and tuned into the classic rock station. Santana's "Black Magic Woman" came in over my headset. He sang about the spell his Black Magic Woman had put on him, and in my solo euphoria, I was immediately convinced that he was singing to me about the spell flying had put on me. I've had a soft spot in my heart for the song ever since.

I executed my solo with no problems, and it was just as exhilarating as I thought it would be. When I taxied back to pick up Bill after making the traditional three landings, I tumbled out of the plane like an excited five-year-old, pulling my pants back on and laughing with glee.

A LONG TIME AGO—BACK BEFORE THEY HAD RADIOS AND headsets in planes, back at the dawn of aviation, when all planes were configured for tandem seating and instructors sat behind their students—an instructor would tug at his student's shirttail to get his attention and then yell what he needed to say. It became tradition for the instructor to cut off the student's shirttail after their first solo, the idea being that they would no longer need to tug on it mid-flight.

That tradition still holds today, and many flight schools hang up the snipped shirttails with the student's name, the date of their solo, the airport where it took place, and perhaps something else noteworthy about the flight written on it by the instructor in permanent marker. Ever since Bill had decided I was ready to solo, I'd been carrying a Hawaiian shirt around in my flight bag: I wanted my shirt to stand out on my flight school's wall of plain white T-shirts, and the shirt reminded me of the pilot my family had flown with in Key West—the one with the flip-flop tan lines on his feet. Bill cut off the tail when I put the shirt on after I landed, but he never wrote anything on it or hung it on the wall of the flight school. Weeks later, I found it lying on the floor in our condo, forgotten. I folded it up and stuck it in my wallet, and have kept it there ever since.

Maybe I should have been mad at Bill for forgetting to hang up my shirttail, but I wasn't. It was my recent triumph—my first solo flight—and the trips we took together that I associated with Bill at the time. I thought this magic—flying somewhere, having sex, and then exploring a town I'd never seen before, a place where he knew all the cool places to go—was *his* magic. I didn't understand that it wasn't his at all. This brand of magic belonged to flying; it belonged to anyone who knew how to fly.

But like I said, I didn't understand that—plus Bill had come along right when I needed him. I'd hated my apartment and hadn't felt safe there, and he'd asked me if I wanted to move in right after the second time my apartment was robbed. In my mind, he'd saved me from the unsafe hell in which I was living. I felt like a girl in a fairy tale whose prince had come to rescue her and whisk her away to exotic new lands. And that feeling was strong enough that I was willing to give him the benefit of the doubt. I convinced myself that his sexist comments were just his clumsy way of trying to show off in front of a young woman student whose pants he'd like to get into. Besides, he was a lot of fun—and he was teaching me how to fly.

six | HOLD UNTIL
FURTHER
CLEARANCE

"I haven't been everywhere, but it's on my list."
—SUSAN SONTAG

"If God had intended us to fly, he'd have given us more money."
—UNKNOWN

MOST FLIGHT INSTRUCTORS AGREE THAT IT'S best to fly at least twice a week if you want to earn your pilot's license. The knowledge, movements, and memorized procedures leave you quickly when you don't use them regularly. After years of flying, many of these things become second nature, and you perform them without consciously thinking through each step. But an interruption in flight training can derail the whole shebang, setting you back and sometimes forcing you to undergo extra training to relearn the things you forgot and adding expense to an already-expensive endeavor.

Given all this, you can probably see why I was so upset when I hit yet another speed bump in my road to pilothood. I was finally starting to get past my issues with airsickness, and so far had managed to stay on track despite my long, demanding work weeks, when I went to my gynecologist's office for my annual checkup. I always dread these appointments, as I seem to suffer an inordinate amount of "female trouble." By this point, I had already undergone two cryosurgeries to remove precancerous cells from my cervix—as well as a third procedure that removed an actual chunk of my cervix when those first two didn't do the trick. Each experience had been painful and disgusting, so my dread heading into this checkup was warranted. And this visit—lucky me—brought even more bad news.

After feeling my ovary, the doctor said she was pretty sure I had a large cyst on it, and she sent me for an ultrasound to confirm. I had never heard of doctors using an ultrasound for anything other than pregnancy; I was too embarrassed to tell anyone but my parents and Bill about it. But the ultrasound did what it was supposed to: it not only confirmed the existence of the ovarian cyst, it also showed that it was 11.5 centimeters in diameter—the largest one, my doctor said, that she had ever seen. It was an accomplishment I could have lived without.

That night, I lay down and pushed all around below my navel, not sure exactly where my ovary was but feeling in the general area my doctor had been touching when she got that look on her face that meant "Houston, we have a female problem." I wondered how it was that I couldn't feel this thing inside me that was the size of a softball. Surgery would be necessary to remove it, although my doctor had told me they could do the procedure arthroscopically, meaning that they would make four small incisions (instead of one big one) to get to the cyst. She described the procedure as "minimally invasive." The term got me. Someone was going to stick a knife in me to remove something from one of my organs, and they were calling it *minimally* invasive. It sounded pretty damn invasive to me.

My doctor knew I was taking flying lessons (because it was so much fun that I was telling anyone who would listen about it), and she was careful to tell me that I should stop flying until after the surgery. "If the cyst ruptures," she warned me, "you will be doubled over in pain. You don't want to be up in an airplane when that happens." This news was a major blow. I hadn't been taking lessons for very long, but already I couldn't imagine *not* doing it. So I did two things: I scheduled the surgery for as soon as I could (not out of fear for my health but because I wanted to get back to flying), and, because I'm stubborn and hard-headed, I still went flying before the surgery (but only with Bill, just in case the cyst ruptured and I was in too much pain to fly).

This would be my first major surgery, requiring general anesthesia. I was terrified, and I told Bill many times just how terrified I was, not so much of something going wrong but just of being helpless. He assured me each time that he'd be there with me. After all, he told me, couples had to be there for each other, right? Because of that, when my mom offered to fly out, I told her that there was no need for her to interrupt her life and come all that way.

"I want to be there for you," she said when we spoke on the phone a week before my procedure.

"It's okay, Mom," I said, pacing my living room. "Bill will be there. He'll take care of me."

"But you're having *surgery*," she said, worry in her voice. "I should be there!"

"It's really okay," I said, trying to sound more confident than I felt. "I'm an adult now. And besides, Bill will take good care of me." I still had that "knight in shining airplane fuselage" image of Bill in my mind, left over from when he'd saved me from my scary apartment. I trusted him to save me again.

I could tell my mom wasn't quite satisfied by my reassurances, but she finally just sighed. "Okay," she said. "I won't come. But you call me as soon as you wake up!"

"I will," I promised. "But don't worry. I'll be fine. Everything's taken care of."

THE DAY BEFORE MY SURGERY, BILL WANTED TO TAKE my mind off of worrying and the necessary pre-surgery fasting that had me famished, so he asked if I wanted to go for a ride around the hills south of San Francisco, close to where we lived. He knew I loved going for car rides, and I thought it was super sweet and thoughtful of him to offer. We picked up his brother, Charlie, who lived near us, and headed out on the road.

We were driving through a beautiful stretch of forest, and I was just taking a deep breath of the eucalyptus-scented air when Bill got a call.

He glanced at his phone. "It's one of my students," he said. "I've gotta get this." He chatted with the person on the other end of the line for a minute or so, and then I heard him say, "Yeah, man, I'll pick you up from SFO tomorrow and we'll go flying in the afternoon."

I couldn't believe it. He knew my surgery was the next day. As soon as he hung up, I told him, "You get back on that phone and you tell him you will absolutely NOT be there!"

"You'll be unconscious," he said defensively. "You won't even need me until after the surgery. I'll have plenty of time to go flying!"

"My doctor said the surgery will only last about an hour," I reminded him. "That's not even close to enough time for you to pick up your student from SFO, drive down to San Carlos, go flying, and get back before I wake up!"

Looking like a wounded puppy, Bill called his student back. "Um, hey, man," he said quietly. "Lemme call you back later."

I fumed for the rest of the car ride, stuck somewhere between furious and hurt. If anyone could understand the pull of flying, it was me. But Bill was supposed to be my partner. How could he consider abandoning me like that, especially when he knew how scared I was?

That night, I woke up vomiting violently; the pre-surgical medications my doctor had put me on were making me sick. Bill had to rush me to the emergency room, where they gave me medication to stop the vomiting.

Once I was stable, a nurse went through the pre-surgery prep with me while Bill sat and listened.

"You'll have to remove your contact lenses," she told me.

"Isn't there any way for me to keep them in?" I asked. I hated taking out my contacts. All I can see without them are blurry masses, so I always use the twenty-four-hour kind that you only have to change once a month.

"Sorry," the nurse said, giving me a sympathetic smile. "They'll have to come out."

I did have glasses back at the condo to use as a backup. I hated them, but wearing them was better than being practically blind, and we only lived about ten minutes from the hospital.

I looked at Bill. "You know I can't see anything without my contacts in," I said. "Will you run home when I go into surgery and bring them back so I'll have them afterward?"

"Sure thing," he said, giving my hand a squeeze.

They wheeled me off a couple minutes later.

"Love you," he called after me. "I'll be right back with your glasses!"

I WOKE UP A COUPLE OF HOURS LATER FEELING VERY groggy and nearly blind. There was a nurse in the room, but Bill was nowhere in sight.

"Could you please go get my boyfriend from the waiting room?" I asked her. "He should be out there."

She came back a minute later. "I'm afraid the waiting room is empty," she said, shrugging.

"That's not possible," I said. "He has to be out there." I sent her back out with a description of Bill.

She came back a minute later and again assured me that the waiting room was empty.

"Is there more than one waiting room?" I asked, knowing but still not believing that he really had gone flying while I was in surgery. The nurse shook her head. There wasn't. He had. I fell back asleep, unable to resist the anesthesia still in my system.

When I woke up again and repeated the boyfriend search with the nurse, Bill still wasn't there. It had now been about three hours. Finally I asked the nurse for a phone and called my mom, crying my eyes out—which, of course, hurt like hell, because sobbing strained my taped-together abdominal incisions. I was realizing that I should have taken my mom up on coming to San Francisco to be with me. Even if Bill had been there, I still would have been happy to have my mom there—and since he wasn't there, I was kicking myself for talking her out of it. Moms are always a comfort to have around during times like those.

My mom was beside herself when I told her that Bill had gone flying and still wasn't back or even answering his phone. I gave her his brother's name, and she hung up with me, called information to get Charlie's number, and called him to ask if he could come get me. The hospital staff was more than ready to get rid of me and were getting upset that I didn't have a ride.

Charlie was already pushing me out of the hospital in a wheelchair when Bill finally showed up. I looked up at him, tears in my eyes, and couldn't say a word. My heart was broken.

Bill looked down at me. Through the blur of my tears and my impaired, lens-less vision, he was little more than a dark shape in front of me.

"Hi," he said, and that was it. No "sorry." No "I'm so glad you're okay." He didn't ask how I was feeling. He didn't even have my glasses.

We went back to our condo, and Charlie was kind enough to spend the rest of the day with me, helping me get to the bathroom and making sure I took my meds on time. Bill was mad at me for being mad at him, so he wouldn't speak to me or help me in any way. I wasn't sure which hurt worse: my still-oozing wounds or getting the silent treatment from someone who claimed to love me and who had bailed on me when I needed him most. My parents and friends pleaded with me to leave him, telling me that what he had done was an unforgivable breach of trust. But I convinced myself that this was just a hiccup in our relationship. Once I recovered, we would have a talk about our expectations of each other, and I knew we'd be able to fix everything. After all, we shared two great loves: our love for one another and our love for flying. How could I give all that up?

Just as I was feeling good enough to get back in the air, a week after my surgery, I woke up vomiting violently again, and Bill had to rush me back to the emergency room.

Turns out the combination of medication and surgery and the resulting disruption to my normal, uh, bodily functions had given me a raging bowel infection. Ultimately, I ended up spending two full months in recovery, unable to do anything but lie on the couch in misery. All I wanted was to be up in the air—but I couldn't even walk around the block, let alone fly a plane.

Still, my time away from flying was not completely wasted. I studied the ground school books and listened to air traffic live feed on the Internet as often as I could, trying to get used to the radio communications that often intimidate the bejesus out of student pilots. I might be out of commission, but I wasn't about to let that stop me from getting back into flying. Plus, learning aviation-ese meant that Bill and I finally spoke the same language. He liked being able to come home after a long day of flying for the airline, plop down on the couch in an exhausted heap, say "You won't believe what happened today!", and tell me all about it in excruciating pilot-talk detail. His previous girlfriend hadn't been a pilot, and thus hadn't understood any of his flying jargon, but with me he could talk about super-complicated instrument approaches, argue about aviation laws, and bitch about the ins and outs of professional piloting, and I could actually make sense of it all. I might never reach his level of flying expertise, but I could at least hold my own in a conversation about it. In many ways, that brought us closer.

What *didn't* bring us closer was Bill's frustration with the changes that had occurred in the airline world in the previous few years, and his resulting cheapness. Before we met, he had been a pilot for one of the "legacy" carriers, was a captain on a Boeing 757 and 767, and "held a line" for which he flew eight days per month to either Hawaii or Paris (versus being on call and never knowing his schedule in advance). It was the perfect pilot life, and he had worked hard to get it. After 9/11, however, the airlines had been forced to furlough a number of pilots, and Bill had gone from having high seniority to being nearly at the bottom of the seniority list.

To better understand airline seniority, let's say an airline has a thousand pilots. If you're in the top five hundred, you're likely a captain and have a good monthly flying schedule. Then something like 9/11 occurs, forcing the airline to furlough 400 pilots to make up for the routes that have just been cut. If you were in the top half before, you may not be now, and even if you haven't been furloughed, you're likely being relegated to piloting a smaller plane and having a less desirable schedule. To make matters even more complicated, as a commercial pilot, it's not the number of years of experience you have or number of hours of flying time you've logged that gain you seniority—it's only your time *at your current company* that matters. So even if you're the #1 senior pilot at one airline, if you decide you want to fly for another airline, you have to start at the very bottom of the seniority list at that new airline. On one hand, I understand this system; on the other, it's a bit ludicrous that a captain is not always the more experienced of the two sitting in the cockpit.

But I digress. My point is that in Bill's case, because of his airline's major furloughs after 9/11 he was now back at the bottom of the seniority list and had gotten knocked down to being a first officer on an MD-80, on call twenty or more days per month. And this meant that many nights/mornings while we were fast asleep, our phone would ring, and both of us knew who it was at that hour. When I picked up the call (the phone was on my side of the bed) and mumbled a groggy "Hello?" I knew I would hear "This is scheduling calling for First Officer Bill." Bill would get in the shower, and I would drag myself out of bed to pack his roll-aboard suitcase for him. He often insisted that he wouldn't make his flight if he had to park the car himself, so I frequently ended up driving him to the airport, eating into the precious few hours of sleep I was getting between days at my own job, where I was working twelve- to sixteen-hour days (an unfortunate but entirely common hazing in the financial industry). This was not exactly the glamorous, dating-an-airline-pilot life I had envisioned—it was more like a blurry, sleep-deprived, alone-most-of-the-time kind of existence.

I could understand why Bill was upset to be back on the bottom again after having paid his dues for so long. I could also understand why he was pissed to have gone from making $120,000 per year as a captain on the 757/767 to making plus or minus $70,000 as an on-call first officer. And on-call commercial pilots are not paid for any time they spend getting to and from the airport—which can be hours in many big airline hub cities—or for the time they spend doing flight preparation and paperwork. They're only paid for the time from when the plane pushes back from the gate to when it lands. So Bill was spending a lot of time "working" and not getting paid for it.

Still, even at his "low" pay of $70,000 per year, Bill was making more money than I was. And yet he was constantly trying to get me to pay more bills than him or a bigger share of *his* mortgage—which, as I told him, was insane, because I was already paying more than I would if I were renting half his condo. And our arrangement was essentially like renting: I knew that money would be gone forever if we broke up, and while I had no plans to leave Bill any time soon, I knew that there were no guarantees when it came to our future together. I paid for expensive house upgrades, California's exorbitant property tax, and all the groceries and utilities, and still Bill demanded more. Every few days, he brought it up; and every time, it turned into a huge fight. One time he even started a fight about it in front of my parents. I should have left him right then and there. But I continued to believe that we could fix our problems because we loved each other, so I continued to ignore the warning signs.

 *seven* | ORION THE
HUNTER

"I may not have gone where I intended to go,
but I think I have ended up where I intended to be."
—DOUGLAS ADAMS

I HAD A FAVORITE PLANE. IT WAS THE ONE I HAD been renting as a student pilot and the one in which I had soloed: I knew it well, and I scheduled it for my lessons whenever it was available. But one day when I went to schedule a lesson online, I found that my favorite plane was no longer available. I went to the airport the next day, and I asked the person at the front desk what had happened to Zero Sierra Papa (airplanes are often referred to by the last three characters of their full six-character identifier). She wasn't sure; I left disappointed.

A month later, however, I noticed that even though Zero Sierra Papa was unavailable for lessons, it was still listed in the club's index of planes for rent. The next time I went to the airport I asked a different front desk person about it, and he said the plane was for sale and was up in Napa now with an airplane broker. Curious, I asked if he had any idea how much they were asking and then wondered why I had even asked that since I was pretty sure I couldn't afford an airplane. He didn't know, but he gave me the broker's number.

I didn't know if an airplane cost five dollars or five million dollars, though I was pretty sure it would be closer to the latter. But it was just after year's end, and—thanks to the numerous professional licenses I'd acquired over the past year—I'd gotten a fairly sizable bonus at work. It was more money than I had ever had at once, and it was, naturally, burning a hole in my pocket. So I called the broker.

"Normally a five-year-old Cessna 172S with GPS would cost around $125,000," he told me, "but because this plane is close to its TBO"—(time before overhaul, when the engine has to be replaced or rebuilt)—"the owner's only asking $100,000."

One hundred thousand dollars. Not five million dollars— but still, more than I had. The broker gave me the name of an airplane loan specialist.

After contacting the loan specialist, I realized that my bonus money was just enough for a down payment. And I could pay for the upcoming engine overhaul—which I could expect to be about $20,000—by adding that amount to my fifteen-year loan, since I couldn't afford that *and* the down payment. I found out I could also keep the airplane available for rent at the flying club, which would help offset my expenses. This plane was never going to pay for itself, but making the whole proposition cheaper in any way sounded good to me.

I was starting to get serious about making this purchase— so, of course, I called my parents, who are just as logical as I usually am. I told them about the plane and about my loan options. Then I asked them what they thought.

After a long pause, my mother said, "Well ... most people buy a house first."

She was right, of course—but this was the Bay Area. "I'll

never be able to afford a house here, Mom," I said. "Even the bad neighborhoods are on another planet from my price range. This plane is something that I can actually afford to buy—and I've never wanted anything this badly."

Sure, this was a little bass-ackwards, but much of life in the Bay Area for me was already that way. By the time we got off the phone, my parents were on board with my plan, albeit a bit cautiously.

I sat down at the kitchen table and crunched some numbers. I didn't own a house, my car was paid off, and I was clawing my way up in the financial world—buying this plane seemed like a pretty safe bet to me. Flying was already taking over my life; I was completely addicted to it. What better way to keep that momentum going than to buy my own airplane, something that I could look after and fly whenever I wanted?

Bill was completely against it—something that I now realize was because he wanted me to spend all my money on him, not on some "silly" aircraft—but it was one thing I was determined to stand my ground on. We argued and argued and argued over me buying that plane—but then again, we argued over everything.

"It's not worth the money," he insisted. "What good are you going to get from it? I'll tell you how much: none. All it's going to be is a hassle. You know how they say boats are just 'holes in the water that you throw money into'? Well I can assure you that planes are even worse."

"You have students who own airplanes," I countered. "Don't they love having their own planes? Wouldn't they say it's worth all the hassle?"

"Sure," Bill said, "but they make four, five, a hundred times more money than you do! For people like us—people who don't make hundreds of thousands of dollars a year—it's just too much time and money. You'll regret buying this plane, I guarantee it." He stomped away.

Bill had been in aviation for all of his adult life and was the son of a career airline pilot; he had lived and breathed aviation since birth. So when he talked about planes, I usually listened, and in this case he damn near swayed me. But there was just something about the thought of owning my own airplane ... I couldn't let it go.

Ultimately, it came down to one huge argument. The broker had called: Someone else was interested in the airplane. I had to decide whether or not to buy within the next twenty-four hours.

After we'd been going back and forth for what felt like an hour, Bill finally said, "Give me ONE GOOD REASON you should own that airplane!"

I thought about it for a second, trying to come up with a logical reason. I couldn't. "I have no good reason," I admitted. "Except that I want to own an airplane ... and it's MY MONEY!"

And, with that, I had made my decision. In the span of less than a week, I went from having a lot of money and never having once seriously thought about owning an airplane to being nearly broke and signing my life away to buy one. It was the biggest impulse buy of my life. I was still a student pilot, meaning I didn't even have my basic private pilot's license yet. Bill was f-u-m-i-n-g, but I couldn't really bring myself to care. I was too excited about MY new airplane.

THE PLANE WAS STILL IN NAPA AT THE BROKER'S AIRPORT office when I bought it, so I had to wait the eternity of a few days until the weekend, when I actually had some free time, to go get it. Bill and I had a pilot friend drop us off at the airport so we could pick it up and ferry it back to its old home at San Carlos Airport, about forty miles south through San Francisco International Airport's airspace.

Bill had told me there was a nice steak restaurant on the field of the Napa airport, so we decided to stay there for dinner (my treat, natch) after our friend dropped us off before picking up the plane. The food turned out to be overpriced and mediocre, but we only fought a little bit over money during the meal, so I was in pretty good spirits when we walked out onto the tarmac to bring my baby home.

The setting that night was so movie-perfect: the sky was clear and starry, and my new plane shone majestically under the constellation Orion. (*Did I see one of those cartoon sparkles flash on the wing and hear angels singing?* I wondered. It sure seemed like I had.) I pointed the constellation out to Bill.

"Wow, look!" I said, squeezing his arm. "Orion! ... Hey that's it! That's the name of my plane!"

And thus was Orion born, even though technically he was already five years old. The name, I hoped, would be fitting beyond just having seen Orion shining above that night. Orion is a hunter, and I imagined my plane and I hunting for adventure together for years to come.

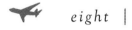 *eight* | A PILOT ONLY
A MOTHER
COULD LOVE

*"I feel about airplanes the way I feel about diets. It seems to me that
they are wonderful things for other people to go on."*
—JEAN KERR, "MIRROR, MIRROR ON THE WALL"

Y PARENTS WERE COMING TO VISIT, AND I really wanted to take them flying in my "new" plane and to show them how special this whole flying thing I couldn't stop talking about was. But my mother hates—loathes—flying. Even in big airliners. So I assumed that my diminutive Cessna wouldn't even be a consideration, especially since I was still just a student pilot.

Given all this, I was very pleasantly surprised, and then a little nervous, when my mother reluctantly agreed to take a dinner flight to Harris Ranch, a cattle ranch in the middle of nowhere (just off I-5 between San Francisco and Los Angeles and about eight miles from the tiny town of Coalinga) that had a steak restaurant. That's about all there is in the area, actually —so much so that all the air traffic controllers for that airspace know that the restaurant's the only reason anyone would fly there and always end their transmission with "Enjoy your steak!" when you get close.

The flight from the Bay Area would give us a view of mountains more than 4,000 feet high—still quite an awe-inspiring sight for a flatlander like me!—and I couldn't wait for my parents to see it. Still, the idea that things might not go as planned made me anxious.

On the evening in question, I crossed my fingers and hoped for my mom's sake that this would be one of those perfectly smooth flights, with not a single bump in the sky.

As we climbed into the plane, I looked back at my mom and smiled. "Remember, Mom, Bill will be sitting right here next to me, and he'll have full access to the controls. This guy has accumulated 16,000-plus hours of flight time—he knows what he's doing!" If that didn't comfort a nervous flier, I didn't know what would.

Her response? "I don't care how many flight hours he has. You are my daughter, and I know you would never kill me."

I stared at her. "But ... Mom. I'm still just a student pilot! That's crazy!"

"I have faith in you," she said. Period.

I couldn't think of a more ridiculous, illogical thing for a person to say ... but I loved her for saying it.

The runway at Harris Ranch Airport is so small—only thirty feet wide—that from the air, it more closely resembles a sidewalk. The wings of even my small plane, with their thirty-six-foot span, hung over its edges. I liked that; it made me feel like I was flying a bigger plane. The smell there, on the other hand, can only be described as unpleasant. Even on approach, while you're still up at altitude, you start to smell cow poo. It does wonders for your appetite just minutes before dinner!

As long as you can stand the smell from the time it hits you in the plane until you've walked the short distance from the airport to the restaurant, Harris Ranch is definitely a great place to enjoy a common pilot pastime: the hundred-dollar hamburger. We pilots love to fly somewhere for lunch on the weekends, and when you add up the cost of fuel—and, for most people, the rental of an airplane—even a five-dollar lunch quickly soars into the triple digits. But that doesn't stop us: the hundred-dollar hamburger is so popular among pilots that there's a book dedicated entirely to listing restaurants located within walking distance from various airports around the country. I love participating in this ritual, as it's a prime example of the adage that travel is not always about the destination itself but also the journey.

On the way back from dinner, once we climbed a bit, my parents got to really enjoy the beauty of flying at night in a small plane. The city lights cascaded out before us, sparkling seemingly just for our enjoyment. San Francisco, there in the distance, was lit up so brightly and so large that we saw it long before we got there, its soft glow illuminating the night sky for miles around.

Thankfully, the flight was smooth both ways, and my mom actually seemed to enjoy herself. I sighed with relief when we landed without incident. I hadn't really thought anything bad would happen, but I was glad that my mom hadn't needed to test her crazy notion that I would never kill her. After all the men I'd seen sneer at women's ability to fly, it was nice to know that someone trusted my piloting abilities so completely—even if she was my mother.

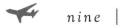 *nine* | THE DEVIL'S
IN THE
DETAILING

"I mingle with my peers or no one,
and since I have no peers, I mingle with no one."
—JOHN KENNEDY TOOLE, *A CONFEDERACY OF DUNCES*

ℳOT LONG AFTER MY PARENTS VISITED, THE GLOW of being a new airplane owner still fresh upon me, I decided it was time to give Orion his first wash and detailing—by me, at least.

It was a typically sunny spring afternoon in California, and I had a rare day off. I stopped at a car parts shop to pick up some cleaning supplies and an industrial brush on a pole so I could reach Orion's wings, and I headed to the airport.

My parking space on the airport grounds didn't have any hoses or other equipment, so I had to taxi the plane to the designated washing area. I got out my cleaning stuff and went to work. Because it was such perfect flying weather, it was a relatively busy afternoon at the airport—and as I scrubbed away, I began to notice that quite a few male pilots were staring at me as they taxied past. I certainly wasn't wearing anything sexy—just running shorts and a T-shirt. I wondered what the big deal was. *Am I doing something wrong?* I gave Orion a once-over. Nothing seemed amiss. What was all the gaping about, then? Hadn't these guys seen a girl wash a plane before?

Then it started. One of the men I had seen stare at me as he taxied past walked over after he had finished tying down his plane.

"Hi, I'm Steve," he said, giving me a friendly wave.

"Hi," I returned. "Erin."

"Is this your plane?" he asked.

"Yep," I responded, "he's all mine!"

"Really?" he said, raising his eyebrows—but he quickly recovered and continued the conversation. Before he left, he offered me his phone number. I took it out of politeness, but that was about it. Whatev. I wasn't there to pick up guys; I was there to wash my plane. So I got back to it.

A few minutes later, another guy walked up and did the same thing. And then another. And another—to the point that I started to get a little frustrated. So many men were interrupting me that more than an hour had passed and I wasn't even halfway through washing my plane! On any other day, the attention would have been welcome—in fact, had my boy-crazy younger self known earlier about this formula for picking up men, I would have scrounged every penny to buy a plane much sooner!—but today I had a mission, and I get super focused when I have a task to complete. It finally clicked for me what was happening when one of the men told me that he'd only seen a few women in aviation, and never a woman so young who owned her own plane. I was a novelty. They'd never seen anything like me before.

I was finally finishing up when yet another guy walked up to me.

Here we go again, I thought.

"Hey, honey," he said, "is this your husband's plane?"

His use of "honey" grated on me, but I decided to ignore it. "No," I said, "I don't have a husband."

"Your boyfriend's, then?"

I understood where he was going now. "No, it's not my boyfriend's," I said, my tone turning a little frosty.

He looked really confused. Finally, he said, "Well, then, whose plane is it?"

"It's my plane," I said flatly.

He almost swallowed his tongue with surprise—but then he laughed like I had just told a funny joke. "No, come on, honey, whose plane is this really?" he insisted.

"Well, *honey*, it really is MY plane, and if you were coming over here to pick up on me, you just blew your chance," I said, turning my back to him. "Move it along," I added over my shoulder before returning my attention to my plane.

When I got home, I called a girlfriend and told her about the veritable parade of men that had come up to give me their phone numbers just because I was washing my plane.

"When are you washing it next?" she asked, laughing. "Can I help?"

I laughed along with her, but it bothered me how many of the guys I'd spoken to that day were *so* surprised that Orion was mine. And that last guy—the one who didn't believe me when I tried to set him straight—really pissed me off. So when I hung up with my friend, I went online and ordered a T-shirt that I had seen advertised in aviation publications before. It read: "No, this is not my boyfriend's airplane." It hadn't really caught my eye in the past, but in light of the day's events, it now held new meaning for me. I wore it to the airport from then on.

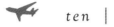 *ten* | INSTRUMENTS
AND AEROBATICS
AND HELICOPTERS
—OH YES!

"Man must rise above the Earth—
to the top of the atmosphere and beyond—
for only thus will he fully understand the world in which he lives."
—SOCRATES

*T*HIS NEWS WILL COME AS NO SURPRISE TO YOU: Bill and I broke up soon after I got my license. He left me for an ex-stripper who looked like she'd been "rode hard and put up wet," as the saying goes—though Bill didn't seem to mind.

We met Crystal on a sailing vacation we took with four other people. This was the whiz kid who, just before our vacation, called the house because she couldn't find her flight at San Francisco International Airport. She knew Bill was a pilot and figured he could give her directions to her gate. Bill, however, was off on a work trip, so I asked if I could help her find it since I knew the airport pretty well. Her flight was to Miami, where she'd stay overnight before heading on to Martinique to meet us. I was pretty sure I knew where the flights for Miami left from.

"Okay, do you know where you are?" I asked. "Or can you at least tell me some shops or restaurants that you see so I can figure out where you are and give you directions?"

"Um ... okay ... so I'm in the international terminal?" she said tentatively back in her valley girl accent.

I sighed and paused, thinking that she'd figure out her mistake as soon as she said the words out loud—but nope, no sign of life.

"Miami is in Florida," I said, hoping the hint would help her out.

Still no sign of life.

"Florida is in the United States."

Again I paused, waiting to hear the figurative face palm. Nothing.

"Since it's in the United States, you'll need to go to the *domestic* terminal, not the international terminal. The international terminal is for flights outside of the United States."

"Oh, okay!" she said brightly. "Thanks! See you in a couple of days!" She hung up.

I was trying to make the most of this trip, even though Bill had given me no say whatsoever in where we went or who came along with us. This brief geography lesson with my boat mate for the next two weeks didn't add to my optimism.

Things only got worse once we were on the boat. Crystal started flirting with Bill from the second our feet hit the boat, and she saw her chance to make a move as we were sailing from St. Lucia to Bequia, while I was nearly lifeless with the worst seasickness I've ever had. They bonded the night that I was so sick I couldn't move. Bill had the night watch, and she stayed up with him to "keep him company." She apparently sealed the deal when I refused to stay on the boat for the reverse trip and opted for the short airplane ride back instead—conditions were worsening, and I just couldn't take it anymore—because she started calling Bill as soon as we got home. He lied about it, of course, and insisted she was calling to thank him for the trip (um … once would be sufficient for that), but it was clear something was going on. I answered when she called the house once, and I told her that Bill and I were still dating and *living together* and asked her to kindly stop calling, and after that he swore she had stopped calling, but I knew better.

It was after Bill came back from a three-day turn with the airline that I finally realized that this little problem, whatever it was, was not going away.

"Just tell me the truth, Bill," I said as he unpacked his bag. "Are you still talking to her?"

"I talked to her once while I was gone," he admitted. "But only because she called me and I felt like I should return her call! Nothing's going on, I swear." He ducked my gaze and headed into the bathroom to take a shower.

Not even a little bit convinced, I checked Bill's phone as soon as he left the room and found that in the past three days, he had called her not once but *thirty-eight* times. It finally hit me: that picture I had of Bill as my white knight was a delusion. He wasn't my savior; he was a liar. And I couldn't live with someone who lied to me.

When Bill walked back into the bedroom in his towel, I confronted him.

I held up his cell phone and at first didn't say a word. He knew I knew.

"So you didn't talk to her, huh? This says you called her thirty-eight times. Bill, you don't call me that much in a year."

That was all I needed to say.

"I kept getting her voicemail, so I kept calling back," Bill tried. But I wasn't buying it.

"Once or twice is sufficient to leave a message if you can't get her. Not thirty-eight times." I was livid but also strangely calm. It was all adding up in my memory now: the surgery stand-up, the not caring when I was sick, the always being late, and finally this—cheating on me with a woman he spent a few days on a boat with. The most important and essentially only person in Bill's life was Bill. I finally got it. It was almost a relief.

"I'll move out as soon as I can find a place," I said. "Just please have the decency to not talk to that woman in my presence."

Bill shrugged. "Fine."

Of course, he didn't keep his word. They had frequent phone conversations, and Crystal even picked him up at the condo once for a date (although she stopped short of ringing the doorbell; she stayed in the car and honked the horn, probably so she didn't have to face my wrath in person). All this made me even more eager to get my own place and get Bill out of my life—the problem was, finding a place in the Bay Area that was below a millionaire's price range was no easy task. I was stuck there for a while before I was able to find something affordable.

Our separation was complicated further because Bill had stopped charging me for flying lessons after we started dating— but now that I'd left, he was threatening to sue me over it unless I repaid the amount, which he calculated to be $4,000, immediately. He even got a lawyer to contact me about it.

I was in no mood for threats, however. I went through my credit card receipts and checking account records and added up everything I had paid for in the time we were together: some of the mortgage, many of the exorbitant property-tax bills, most of the supplies for the renovation of *his* condo, all of the groceries, all of our meals out, and on and on. I was shocked by the total I arrived at.

"Go ahead and sue me," I said. "Feel free. But the minute you do, I'll be countersuing for the $35,000 you owe *me!*" *You do the math there, Sparky.*

I punctuated that sentiment by having my attorney give Bill a call to say the same thing. That shut him up.

LOOKING BACK, I WAS INCREDIBLY NAÏVE THROUGHOUT my relationship with Bill; I couldn't see or think about things clearly while I was in it, and I stayed in it far longer than I should have. Two positive things did come from our relationship, though, and they are big positives: 1) I got my pilot's license under his admittedly excellent tutelage—and my check pilot (an FAA examiner who you have to fly with on a check ride as a final "test" to get your license, much like when a teenager gets her first driver's license and has to take a driving test) even told Bill after our flight that it was one of the cleanest check rides he'd ever given; 2) I learned to look for and recognize certain behaviors in men right away—especially dishonesty and financial insolvency—and to run and not look back when I saw them. This latter lesson has served me extremely well in the years since. It may seem like I'm trying a bit too hard to find the silver lining here—but hell, when a relationship is that utterly disastrous, you need to look for something you gained from it!

Unfortunately, even after moving out of Bill's condo, I wasn't entirely rid of him: we still belonged to the same flying club. We did have pretty much opposite schedules, though, so although we occasionally ran into each other there, we mostly managed to avoid one another. And now that the two of us were through, I began to spread my wings (pun intended) and try new things. Aviation was my drug now, and I was constantly looking for that higher high, that stronger hit. First on my list: getting my instrument rating.

Getting an instrument rating means learning to fly solely by referencing your flight instruments (rather than by looking at the horizon or using anything else that tells you whether you're right side up, upside down, or sideways). Many professional pilots say it's the hardest rating to earn; I liked the challenge it presented. I also knew that getting an instrument rating—or, more precisely, learning those skills that qualified me for one— was pretty much a necessity to keep becoming a better pilot, and would help keep me alive if I ever got myself into a bad situation with the weather—which is too often the cause of fatal accidents in general aviation because it's so unpredictable. Even when you're equipped with all the latest technology, a bad storm can catch you unawares and put you in a bad situation. If that ever happened to me, I wanted to be prepared to deal with it.

Learning to fly just by looking at the cockpit instruments requires wearing some form of hood or glasses that obscure or even completely black out your view outside—otherwise it would be too easy to cheat and glance out the window. I enjoyed the challenge this posed, but it was hard for me to put the hood on during a beautiful day. I was used to keeping my gaze glued to the window, mind immersed in the scenery. My new instructor, Brad, knew that it frustrated me to miss out on the views, so he frequently taunted me about it ("Oh! You wouldn't believe how nice it is today!"; "Wouldn't you just *love* to see outside?").

I breathed a sigh of relief when I finally earned my instrument rating and got to set aside the hood for good. I was excited to have the rating, but the whole thing was way too rules-oriented for me. I loved flying for the freedom it allowed me—and that included getting to check out the scenery whenever I felt like it.

NEXT ON MY HIGHER-HIGH LIST WAS AEROBATICS. Aerobatics is basically stunt flying—doing loops, rolls, spins, and many more exciting maneuvers with your plane. My instructor for this discipline was Randy, a friend of mine and one of the most colorful instructors at my flying club. A consummate New Yorker, Randy had been a cab driver before he was a flying instructor, and he had seen and heard just about everything—which, in turn, meant that no matter what the topic, he had a strong opinion to offer and did so freely. He was short-tempered and easily incited, too—he had already been kicked off the instructor staff at one flight school for having a heated argument with the chief pilot—but he had a heart of gold. And his frothing-at-the-mouth rants were always highly entertaining to witness.

Beyond his many wonderful personal attributes, Randy had a lot of rich students who owned nice aerobatic planes—and once I started training with him, I got to fly them! Just one problem: my old enemy, airsickness, came back with a vengeance during my first lesson. I was only able to stand about thirty minutes of aerobatics before we had to fly back to the airport.

I'd been doing so well with motion sickness lately—it came and went, but mostly I hadn't been feeling it when I flew. So it was a huge blow to find myself getting so sick so fast while I was up in the air with Randy. I knew, however, that overcoming it was just a matter of building up a tolerance to it. I stuck with it.

I was also slowly building up a tolerance for G loads. A G load is a multiple of the normal effect of gravity that is experienced in flight maneuvers; we experience a G load of 1G just by being on earth, but anything above 1G makes you feel heavier. (A 100-pound person, for example, will feel like they weigh 200 pounds in a 2G load, and so on.) Some of the aerobatic maneuvers Randy was teaching me required pulling 4Gs, so that was something I had to train my body to get used to.

When you pull a lot of positive G, all your blood rushes to your lower extremities; sitting there, my entire face sagging, my boobs getting way too close to my waist, and my shoulders and back hunching over, I sometimes wondered if I was experiencing what it feels like to be an old woman. Negative G, meanwhile, offers the opposite feeling: it pulls you up from your seat and sends all your blood to your head.

Negative G is the more dangerous force, and therefore the human body can sustain much less negative G than positive G. You can somewhat combat the effects of positive G by squeezing your lower muscles as hard as you can, forcing blood back up into your torso and head (this is what a fighter pilot's "G suit" does for him: it squeezes his legs). But for negative G, there's no way to squeeze your head to force the blood back down—which is probably why pulling a lot of negative G makes you feel like your head is going to explode from the sudden pooling of blood.

The first few times, pulling a G load basically just made me feel very sick. With positive G, one second, I had normal vision; the next, all peripheral vision was gone but this one tiny dot in the middle—"tunnel vision." And it scared the crap out of me! With negative G, meanwhile, the blood pooling in my head gave me a very sudden and intense headache. "And you pay good money for this?!" you're probably thinking. But luckily, my tolerance for G forces increased with practice, and I became increasingly addicted to the feeling. In time, one of my favorite things about aerobatics was the feeling of my ponytail and necklace standing straight up (or down, as the case might be) when we flew inverted. I also found it really cool, and quite a surprise, how difficult it was to turn my head to check that we were perpendicular to the horizon when we pulled into a vertical up line (where the airplane is positioned straight up). Gravity is shockingly powerful when you start to multiply its force—a fact you can only fully appreciate when you've experienced it firsthand.

The other thing I loved about aerobatics training were all the new entries peppering my logbook. After each lesson, I sat down and documented the different aerobatic maneuvers we had just worked on: barrel rolls, snap rolls, shark tooths, hammerheads, Cuban 8s, Immelmans, tail slides, humpties, knife edges, lazy eights—the whimsical names lent poetry to my otherwise very businesslike logbook.

My favorite maneuver, hands down, will always be the full Cuban 8. To perform one, you start in level flight, then pull up to execute a loop—but once you are over the top of the loop and pointed 45 degrees down, still inverted, you hold the angle for a few seconds, and then—still pointed 45 degrees down—do a half roll so you're right side up. Then you pull up into a loop and do the exact same thing on the other side. The figure you cut with the move looks similar to the infinity symbol but with a flat bottom and flattened lines converging in the middle—very cool looking. But the real reason I liked it was because I got to both go inverted and do a half a roll on each side (the full rolls kind of screwed with my head—the horizon did a full 360

during those, and that made my airsickness come on quicker—
so I tried to avoid those).

Top-quality aerobatic airplanes are built to sustain more G
load than my body—or most bodies—could ever hope to
handle. And as you might expect, they're not cheap. I got access
to some very nice planes through Randy, including a Pitts
Special, but when I met a guy through my flying club who
owned an Extra 300L, I realized there was little I wouldn't do to
get a chance to fly it.

The Extra 300L is used by many world-champion–caliber
aerobatic pilots. It is a small, low-wing airplane with a clear
canopy instead of a roof, and it sits two people, one in front of
the other. This arrangement is called "tandem" seating (like on
a tandem bicycle). The plane also has a "conventional" gear
configuration (as opposed to a "tricycle" gear configuration,
which is what most planes have today)—there is a small wheel
on the tail (known as a tailwheel) and two main wheels in front,
so the plane tilts up when it is sitting on the ground. Conventional-gear airplanes take a lot more finesse to maneuver
than tricycle-gear planes because the tail can be pushed around
by the wind, making landing in a crosswind rather tricky. But
since the tailwheel is smaller than the nose gear in a tricycle-
gear configuration, it offers less drag and is therefore more
aerodynamic, which is why aerobatic planes still have this configuration: most pilots are willing to put up with a little drag in
the interest of ease of use, but aerobatics pilots are not.

Because of all these differences, when I was learning
aerobatics, I had to go through more basic training (read: landings, landings, landings) to get used to the tailwheel configuration. Sometimes even taxiing felt difficult when the tail
was getting pushed around in the wind. I had definitely become
very spoiled by my user-friendly Orion! But I was also deter-

mined to be able to fly pretty much any small plane I laid my eyes on, so I kept at it. And I loved the Pitts Special: it is also a conventional-gear airplane, but it has added sex appeal—to me, at least—because it's a biplane. Even better, the one I got to fly had a dreamy paint scheme of stripes and stars that made it look like a superhero's plane.

Still, I had never flown an Extra 300L, and I was dying to give it a whirl. So when my aerobatic instructor introduced me to a guy who owned one, I started flirting with him. It had been nine months since my breakup with Bill, and I still wasn't quite all there emotionally—in that short time, I'd gone through five lovers. I was enjoying my newfound freedom, but was taking advantage of it a bit too ... freely. I temporarily entertained the idea of dating this guy after he took me to the business he owned, I guess to show off a bit. I wasn't sure how to react as he walked me around the warehouse and introduced me to some of his employees; it was mostly just kind of awkward. I invited him to join me and my friends on a pilots' night out once, too— but I really wasn't that interested in him, just his airplane. And he kept saying we could go fly his plane soon, but after a few of those "promises," I got the feeling he was holding out the flight for sex. So I slept with him. Just so I could fly his airplane. Not my finest moment—but what a plane!

If this whole interlude sounds unceremonious, it's because it was! My love life after my breakup with Bill was a bit like flying aerobatics: fly a maneuver, right the airplane, check the instruments, go right into the next maneuver and repeat ... except in this case, each "maneuver" was a new lover. It would be a while before I left this phase behind.

THE NEXT THING I TURNED TO IN AN ATTEMPT TO SATE my ever-increasing need for an aviation fix was learning to fly helicopters. Few pilots fly both fixed-wing and rotary-wing aircraft because safety habits developed in one type can actually be dangerous habits in the other. Mastering helicopters also requires a whole new understanding of the physics of flying. Think about it like this: when an airplane's engine quits for any reason, it doesn't just fall out of the sky, as many people fear; rather, it becomes a glider. Admittedly, some planes glide better than others, but none will just plummet out of the sky. My fixed-wing instructors always told me, "An airplane essentially wants to fly, so just let it do its thing." And it's true. If you have an airplane "trimmed up" correctly—if the controls are set for level flight—it will go on flying until the fuel runs out, even if the pilot passes out or dies.

Not so for a helicopter. Helicopters require a strange, spastic-looking dance of all four limbs moving seemingly at random, the operation of which makes the pilot look a bit like a drunken octopus. Both of your feet must constantly make small corrections on the rudders, which control the tail rotor for anti-torque; you use your left arm to move the collective, which controls the pitch of the blades on the main rotor; your left wrist twists the throttle to control RPM; your right arm moves the cyclic, the stick that comes up from the floor, to control the main rotor tilt for direction of flight; and your head constantly pivots as you check your instruments on your left (the helicopter pilot sits on the right side of the aircraft, as opposed to fixed-wing pilots, who sit on the left)—and, of course, look outside and down at the amazing view the canopy bubble offers.

In airplanes, the instrument panel often comes up to just above my eye level; in many cases I have to sit up and stretch my back to see over it. Helicopters, in contrast, have only a small instrument panel in the middle, which sits at about knee level. Everything else is a big window, from the roof down to the floor. It was a whole new perspective, and when I first started flying helicopters, I kept getting transfixed by everything I could see in front of and under me. The first time I flew a helicopter, in fact, I was so mesmerized by the panoramic view that for a few seconds I forgot I was flying! It's not just that the canopy bubble offers a more complete vista than an airplane's windshield—it's that there are no wings below you or above you to block anything out. Plus, the diminutive Robinson R22 helicopter I was flying—a two-seater designed for small people —looked like a dragonfly in flight, and it gave me the sensation of hanging in the sky rather than riding a tin can through it. And so I became addicted to the additional beauty offered by rotary-wing flight.

But like I said, when a helicopter's engine quits, it doesn't become a glider; it drops like a rock. So once I'd gotten the basics of helicopter flying down, then came the thrill of doing practice autorotations. It's an emergency maneuver only, but it's one that you have to learn to the point that it becomes reflex: you jam the collective down to keep you from spinning out of control from the torque, and just before you hit the ground you execute a flare and use the pressure of the air that you just forced down under you to "catch" you. As if that weren't stressful enough, you have to initiate an autorotation within about two seconds of the engine quitting, because beyond that point the torque of the still-turning main rotor will spin the fuselage out of control.

So there's no room for that moment of "Holy shit, did my engine just quit?"—that is a luxury of fixed-wing flight. When the engine quits in a helicopter, you had better be trained to reflexively slam down the collective before you spin out of control. There's no looking all around as you glide, searching for the best place to land; you are coming down, and you're not going to land far from where you started. You just have to cushion the fall before you hit. And if you do time that flare just right, you will only "fall" from a foot or two above the ground, which means you can still enjoy a soft landing.

After endlessly practicing autorotations, hovering in crosswinds, and executing landings, landings, and more landings in a helicopter, I still had to fulfill the same requirements I had completed for my fixed-wing license, including solo flights, cross-country flights (flights to two different airports at least forty nautical miles away), solo cross-country flights, and night flights.

During one of my solo cross-countries, I landed at Marina Airport just north of Carmel, California, and while I was fueling up the helicopter (the small R22 I was training in did not hold much fuel, so it was necessary to refuel on even my fairly short cross-country), a guy came over to talk to me.

"What are you doing here?" he asked—but in a curious way, not in an ugly way.

It was a quiet airport, so I took his question at face value and decided to be friendly. "I'm a student helicopter pilot on my solo cross-country," I told him. "I fly airplanes, too, but I just started flying helicopters recently."

"I've been a helicopter pilot for more than forty years, and I have never seen a woman fly a helicopter before," he said, scratching his head. "I couldn't believe it when I saw this R22 land and then saw you hop out!" He looked impressed.

"There are more of us out there than you might think!" I said.

"I suppose there must be!" he said, and he gave me a broad smile. "Well, best of luck to you! I hope I see you back here again soon."

I laughed and shook his hand before climbing back into the helicopter.

When I got back from that flight, I immediately sought out the owner of the helicopter flight school, who was a woman, and found her talking with another instructor (who also happened to be a woman). When I told them what the guy at Marina Airport had said, we all had a good laugh about it.

 *eleven* | ROAD (AIR) TRIP!

"The ships hung in the sky in much the same way that bricks don't."
—DOUGLAS ADAMS, *THE HITCHHIKER'S GUIDE TO THE GALAXY*

*F*OR THE PAST ALMOST TWO YEARS, ALL I'D DONE was eat, sleep, drink, talk, and dream about aviation in all its wonderful manifestations and glory—so I couldn't wait to attend my first aviation convention. For my first experience, I chose the annual convention held by the Aircraft Owners and Pilots Association (AOPA), the national general aviation advocacy association that promotes safety and community involvement. AOPA has more than 400,000 members and holds a great convention every year that features airplanes on display, all kinds of aviation-related retailers exhibiting their coolest stuff, safety seminars, roundtable discussions, and symposia on numerous topics. The convention that year—2006—was to be held over a long weekend in early November in Palm Springs, California.

My flying club friends and I had been planning our trip for about a week, figuring out who was going with whom and which planes we were taking. The only problem was Ron.

Ron was a guy who belonged to the flying club—I'm sure

there's someone like this in all flying schools and clubs, the same way all families have one really eccentric aunt or uncle—who was on so much medication for his mental and emotional issues that he couldn't legally become a pilot. So he was forever sentenced to being only a student pilot, forced to fly with an instructor at all times. The instructors were constantly passing him off to any new, unsuspecting teacher who came along. I felt bad for the guy. But he had developed a thing for me after he heard that Bill and I were no longer together, and if he hadn't been hard enough to be around to begin with, his newfound crush had made him pretty much insufferable.

This was yet another time when I was reminded of what a minority I was in as a female pilot. I didn't see any of the female pilots following the male pilots around like puppy dogs, but the reverse was not uncommon. Don't get me wrong—I don't mind a little male attention every now and again—but there's a line between attention and harassment, and in this case, that line was getting pretty blurry. For example: One day while I was sitting at the airport café enjoying a peaceful lunch alone, sitting by the window and reading, Ron saw me there and came in and sat down at my table and then wouldn't stop talking. I tried to interrupt to tell him that I only had a finite amount of time to read and that I'd really like to be left alone, but I couldn't get a word in. He'd latched on, and he wouldn't let go.

Of course, it was impossible to keep a trip like this a secret at the flying club. Ron soon found out through the grapevine that we were all going to Palm Springs, and he wanted in. He *really* wanted to be with me—and beyond that (understandably, I admit), he wanted to feel like he was part of the flying community. But I didn't want him anywhere near this trip. I had taken so little vacation for years, and was still only recently out of my two-year relationship with Bill; I was planning to have an absolute blowout of a time on this trip. But I knew that if Ron was there—shadowing me everywhere, waiting for his chance to get me alone—I wouldn't be able to let go the way I wanted to. I'd painted a rosy picture of what this weekend was going to look like, and Ron simply wasn't in it.

Once Ron found out exactly who was going to Palm Springs, he started trying to bum a ride—starting with me, since he knew I would be flying my plane there and taking only my new roommate and recent instrument instructor, Brad. Ron could do the math. A four-seater plane with only two people. He sidled up to me in the club one afternoon to make his case.

"Hey Erin!"

"Hi," I responded, groaning inwardly.

"So I heard you guys are going to Palm Springs ... think I could bum a ride with you?" he asked.

At least he got straight to the point.

"Sorry Ron, we don't have room," I said, shrugging. "It's just me and Brad, but I'm taking a ton of luggage—we're going to be too heavy as it is." *Lie.* But what else could I do? I wasn't going to let this guy ruin my perfect weekend.

"I can fit," Ron argued. "I'll barely bring anything, I promise!"

"I'm sorry," I said firmly. "You know how important weight is. You'll put us over the limit. It's just not possible."

Ron knew as well as anyone that you can't argue with the PIC—Pilot in Command—so he gave up and went off to beg elsewhere. Luckily, my aerobatics instructor was taking his wife in his two-seater bush plane, so Ron couldn't go with them either, and he didn't get a bite with any of the other pilots he asked (many of whom he didn't even know), either. *Phew. Crisis averted.*

On the morning we were to leave, I drove to the airport and walked out to my plane—only to see Ron sitting in a plane parked right next to mine.

I'm usually too nice a person to say flat out what I really think about someone, but I could see he was going to test my niceness that day. He was sitting there on purpose, in hopes of running into me. As I walked nearer, I saw that he was sitting behind the yoke (the plane's "steering wheel") and playing with it and looking at the instruments, the way kids do when you show them an airplane. I was waiting to hear him emit a "Vrooooom!"

There was no way to avoid him; I decided to just deal with him and get it over with.

"What are you doing, Ron?" I said, halfheartedly trying to keep the irritation out of my voice.

"Dry flying," he said matter-of-factly.

Dry flying. Hmm. I had never heard that term before. I told myself I should just excuse myself politely and walk away, but the guy pushed my buttons. I couldn't help myself. "Dry flying?" I repeated. "Is that like dry humping?"

Without waiting for his response, I walked away to preflight my airplane.

THE FLIGHT FROM SAN FRANCISCO DOWN TO PALM Springs took us over California's gorgeous, widely varying terrain. Leaving the Bay Area, we first flew over lush green mountains; then the terrain flattened out and turned brown; then it morphed into barren desert before climbing back up into mountains again. The Mojave Desert was surreal; the land below us looked more like the surface of Mars than anything here on earth. As we continued on, the gigantic (12,500-foot) Mojave Airport runway—where Burt Rutan's company, Scaled Composites, one of the first players in the civil aviation space race, is based, and from which his SpaceShipOne-carrying White Knight took off—unfolded before us. Beyond that, in the same valley, we spotted Edwards Air Force Base, with its 15,000-foot runway and dry lakebed overrun, which was used as a backup for space shuttle landings in the past. We couldn't get as close to these landmarks as I would have liked, because they're near a section of military-use-only airspace—but it's hard to miss a 15,000-foot runway! To put things in perspective, most runways I had landed on were anywhere from 2,000 to 5,000 feet. I was sure I could easily land sideways (as in, perpendicular to the runway alignment, not with my airplane sideways—that would be bad news on any runway!) on that thing and have room to spare.

Brad and I arrived in Palm Springs in the early afternoon, and once we checked in we lazed around by the pool all day and well into the evening, hanging out with other friends who arrived throughout the day. After hours of listening to me talk about going swimming but not actually doing it, my friends talked me into getting in the water.

"C'mon, Erin," Brad urged. "Just do it!"

So I dove in—and immediately realized my mistake. This was the first time I'd gone swimming since switching to contacts from glasses, and the second my face hit the water, both of them came out. *Crap.*

I knew there was no way to find them. And I was on my last pair, so I didn't have any spares. *Double crap.* I hauled myself out of the water and grabbed my towel and clothes.

"I'm going to call it a night, guys."

"Where are you going?" Brad asked. "It's still early!"

"I'm pretty tired," I lied, and quickly made my exit. The truth was, I knew I was going to have to wear my glasses now, and I was embarrassed. Beyond the problem of aesthetics, I hadn't had my prescription updated once I switched to contacts, so I wasn't sure how well I would see, even with my glasses on. As I walked back to our room, I comforted myself with the thought that all it would take to remedy the situation was a simple phone call to my contacts retailer; they could overnight replacements to me, and I would have them in time to fly us back home.

I woke up early the next morning and went for a run (feeling awkward in my glasses, which by now I was no longer used to). I was amazed at how cold and dry the place was, and how desert-like it looked. I hadn't really pictured anything in California looking so much like New Mexico. The town buildings were even painted earthy colors, so they all blended into their surroundings. It looked so foreign—and so boring—since I'm used to the brightly and often multicolored houses in New Orleans.

Feeling a bit more centered after my run, I took a quick shower and then met up with Brad; we were both anxious to get to the convention. I called my contacts retailer as we walked around airplane displays in a huge parking lot outside the convention center. They insisted they could not overnight a replacement pair without a prescription from my doctor.

Instantly, my good mood was ruined. *Really? What am I going to do? Overdose on contacts?* I really couldn't see the harm in them sending me a replacement pair.

"I'm a pilot," I told the woman on the line, "and I flew down here from San Francisco. I'll have no way to get back home without contacts!" How could they refuse that kind of need?

They did.

Pissed off but still assuming I could fix the situation, I called my doctor back in New Orleans, an old family friend who I was sure would do me this favor. But he refused to write the prescription without giving me a vision test first.

"Your eyesight could have changed since your last test," he said. "I'm sorry, Erin, but I just can't do it."

This was supposed to be a *vacation*. I was still working twelve- to fourteen-hour days—sometimes even longer than that—six days a week. I had even recently spent the night under my desk after a super-long day, as commuting home would have cost me precious sleep. So I needed this break; I didn't want to have to spend the whole time worrying about being able to see my way home!

I tried to pull myself out of my funk. I walked aimlessly around the airplane display, hung out at a friend's makeshift tiki bar nearby, watched a literal parade of airplanes taxi by, and hitched a ride in another friend's airplane so I could be in the parade. A New Orleans girl through and through, I couldn't resist a parade—even if no one was throwing beads—and I figured it would cheer me up. I also hoped it would get my mind off the fact that I was wearing my glasses, which was making me extremely self-conscious at a time when I wanted to be really extroverted.

Then, just when I was starting to enjoy myself, the calls and texts started coming in. *Ron.* He had driven *through the night* to get to Palm Springs—an eight-hour journey, all told—and was now at the convention; he was wondering where I was so he could meet up with me and we could do everything together. The man had driven eight hours to hang out with me, not knowing where I was, where I was staying, or if I'd even answer my phone —which, for the record, I didn't. But now everywhere I went, I was jerking my head around, afraid I'd run into Ron and be stuck with him for the weekend. And since I couldn't see very well with those damned glasses on, I was afraid he would spot me before I saw him coming and engaged in evasive maneuvers.

I knocked out early again that day, tired of playing the

mouse to Ron's cat, and walked back to the hotel, where I joined my friends for dinner and answered their questions about how many times Ron had called and texted. The number was still growing; at the beginning of dinner, we were up to thirty-nine, but by halfway through the meal their frequency had begun to wane. Maybe he was finally getting it. *Sorry you drove all night, dude, but you can't just assume I wanna be your convention date.*

My bad mood and Ron's barrage of texts and calls led me to drink way too much. *Way* too much. And I seldom drink, so I don't handle it well when I do. I ended up sleeping through the convention the next day, laid low by a combination of still feeling hung over and not wanting to risk having Ron see me and latch onto me. I got the report about the convention goings-on from Brad that evening, we had another dinner out with our friends (much less festive this time—no drinking for me), and then I went to bed early. I had enjoyed the convention, but I enjoyed the flying more; I wanted to be sure I was well rested for the return trip.

We got to the airfield early Monday morning and started our preflight check.

"How are those glasses?" Brad asked. "Can you see okay?"

I tested them out, and found that despite their slight out-dated prescription, my glasses allowed me to see distance clearly, and I therefore could see well enough to fly. I gave Brad the thumbs-up. "They're okay!"

As we and our other friends prepared for takeoff, someone had a brilliant idea: "Why don't we fly formation back to the Bay Area?"

Flying formation involves two or more airplanes flying in close proximity. *How* close can vary—it can range anywhere from a foot and a half, like the Blue Angels do, to ten or twenty feet like the rest of us flying mortals do. Mostly it depends on how comfortable the pilots feel with one another. No one in our group was quite at Blue Angels level, so we decided we'd leave a good fifteen to twenty feet between us during the flight.

There were three planes in all: my Cessna, my aerobatics instructor's Decathlon, and another friend's Decathlon. Previously, I had only flown formation with other Cessnas like mine, where we all flew at the same speed and could use normal cruise-power settings—but Decathlons are a bit slower than Cessnas, so for this flight, done in a standard triangle formation, I had to throttle way back. Your neck gets stiff flying formation because you have to remain in one position, always looking out the window at the plane closest to you, so we switched positions once in a while to give ourselves a chance to move our heads another way. Those position changes were the best part of the flight—swooping under the other planes, seeing the oil-streaked underbelly that seldom gets cleaned as I reduce power to sink under the other plane and gently bank, keeping both eyes fixated on it in case we get too close. Once on the other side, you add a hint of power back to climb back up, and it looks like a mirror image of where you just were seconds ago. The scenery was also spectacular, of course—shifting from mountainous desert to flat desert and then to green mountains —but as my gaze was glued to the airplane next to me, I only got to see it from the corner of my eye.

After an hour or so in the air, we stopped at General Fox Airport, just outside Palmdale—the older pilots' bladders weren't as resilient as mine, and we were ready for lunch. After eating, since the runway was plenty wide enough (150 feet across) to accommodate it, we executed a formation takeoff—my first ever. A formation takeoff is what it sounds like: the planes in your group take off together from the runway, already positioned how they will be in the air, rather than taking off one by one and then joining up in the air, as we had done earlier.

As we continued along our route, I made a point of ending each initial contact with the air traffic controllers we passed with "flight of three" to let them know we were in formation. I was tempted to add, "'Cause that's how we roll!"—but I refrained, though it wasn't easy to do so. I was feeling more and more like a Blue Angel—a slower version, sure, but equally cool.

After such a perfect day of flying, I was disappointed when we got to our home control area of NorCal approach. I didn't want the day to end, especially knowing that it was back to work for me the next day. It hadn't been the perfect vacation I had hoped for, but I had made some great memories—and I had ended it on a high note. And I'd even managed to avoid Ron.

 *twelve* | CLEARED
FOR
TOUCH AND GO

*"Flying an aeroplane with only a single propeller to keep you in the air.
Can you imagine that?"*
—CAPTAIN JEAN LUC PICARD, STAR TREK: THE NEXT GENERATION

ETWEEN MY FIRST AIRPLANE WASH ATTRACTING every guy on the field and Ron's intrastate stalking, I was finally catching on to the fact that being a woman in aviation—and a young one, at that—definitely drew a fair share of men. So rather than continuing to be an unwitting target, I decided to turn that fact to my advantage.

I flew to Davis, California to go on my first blind date ever, set up by a pilot friend for his pilot friend. We hit it off instantly and stayed up all night after dinner just talking. Yes, *just talking.* Our mutual friend, Nick, often referred to my date as "Wingman" because he was often his actual wingman during flights and would also play that role when they went to bars together, so I immediately started using the name as well.

Wingman owned a very demanding construction business and worked pretty much around the clock, so his driving or even flying to the Bay Area to see me was out of the question. I can see how that might have been a deal-breaker for some women, but I didn't mind—I always liked a good excuse to fly! So I would fly the half hour to Davis from Silicon Valley, or, if the weather was really bad, I would drive (all the while marveling at how much longer it took!) in order to spend time with Wingman. Whenever I did, he would stop working at least long enough to show that he also wanted to spend time with me.

We only dated for a month, but his birthday happened to fall during that period, and I wanted to give him a one-of-a-kind gift.

"I want to do something special for your birthday," I told him a week before the big day.

"What kind of something special?" he asked.

"You'll have to wait and find out," I said, giving him a wink. "But flying will be involved!"

He tried getting more details out of me, but I wouldn't budge, and finally he gave up asking.

The afternoon of his birthday, I drove us to the airport.

"Are we going to dinner somewhere?" he asked, getting curious again.

I just shrugged and smiled. "You'll find out soon enough!"

Once we were in the air, I headed straight for the most remote and empty airspace I could think of, turned on the autopilot, and had him attend to the controls while I attended to his "present."

When we were back on the ground in Davis and securing the airplane, I looked at Wingman and smiled. "So, how cool was your birthday present?" I asked.

"You're the best girlfriend EVER!" he responded, laughing.

Unfortunately, he went and ruined things a couple of weeks later by giving me a card that said "I love you" just before I left for a trip home to see my parents. As soon as I read the card, I started to freak out. *I love you?* I thought, shocked. *How can anyone fall in love with someone in such a short time?* I didn't believe they could—and besides, I wasn't exactly looking for love yet. My relationship with Bill wasn't out of my system yet. Love hurt, so I was looking to avoid it for the time being. Besides, I thought there had to be something wrong with him for falling in love so fast. So I bailed. I came home from Louisiana, and promptly broke up with Wingman.

THE NEXT MAN I DATED, MITCH, DIDN'T LAST LONG either, and for a similarly ridiculous reason. Yep, the same person who stuck with a chauvinistic pig for two years was suddenly ready to give any guy the boot the second he made the wrong move. I guess you could say I went from one extreme to the other!

Mitch was deaf, and wore a cochlear implant so he could hear. At night, however, he removed the magnet part of the receiver he wore just behind his ear to go to sleep, making himself completely deaf. The one night I spent at his place, he forgot to mention one tiny detail about how he would wake up in the morning—and since an aural alarm is something I take completely for granted, when I saw him set his alarm before we went to sleep, I didn't stop to think, "How will he hear that?"

The next morning, I jolted awake to the feeling of the bed shaking really hard under me.

Oh no, this is the Big One! I thought, and I bolted to the window. How bad was it? Were the buildings around us going to shake apart?

Meanwhile, Mitch groggily opened his eyes and then reached over to turn off his "alarm." The shaking stopped.

I sagged back against the window. "I seriously almost just had a heart attack!" I said, throwing my hands up.

Mitch just shook his head. He couldn't hear me. He reached for his receiver and put it back on his ear. "What did you say?" he asked.

"I said, I almost had a *heart attack!* Why didn't you tell me about your alarm?" I asked.

He shrugged. "I guess I thought you'd figure it out."

Mitch's shaky alarm clock wasn't the reason I broke up with him, however. It was how he treated my airplane. Every time I took him flying, no matter how many times I told him not to, he slammed the door of my airplane. I mean *slammed*—as in, he'd nearly impale the door on the latch. I showed him how to close it gently. Multiple times. But he just didn't get it. And after a few more times, I snapped.

"I can't do this anymore."

Mitch just looked at me for a moment. "What?" he finally asked.

"You and me. I think we should see other people."

"But why?" he asked, rubbing the back of his neck. "Things are going so well!"

"Honestly?" I asked. "Because you won't stop slamming the door of my plane."

"Because *what?*" Mitch asked, his eyes widening in disbelief.

"It's not just that. But yes, that's a big part of it."

"You've gotta be kidding," he said.

But I wasn't. And that was the end of Mitch.

These reasons for ending relationships may sound flimsy, but beneath the seemingly superficial reasons I had for breaking up with Wingman and Mitch was a much deeper meaning: I was learning, slowly, what type of treatment I would and would not accept—and my plane, which I now considered to be part of myself, was a part of that equation. Slowly but surely, I was reclaiming my sense of self. And while my reactions were perhaps a bit extreme in these cases, I was at least getting closer to knowing what I wanted in a relationship.

And besides, when someone I take flying is too rough with the door of my plane now, I can say, completely honestly, "I broke up with a guy once for slamming it that hard!" And what do you know, they get the picture and stop doing it.

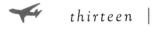 *thirteen* | RETURN TO
BASE (RTB)

"When preparing to travel, lay out all your clothes and all your
money. Then take half the clothes and twice the money."
—SUSAN HELLER

"I did not leave my heart in San Francisco."
—ME

IT HAD BEEN COMING FOR YEARS NOW, ARGUABLY
since the first day I walked to my new job and found
the people in the office building so rude: it was time to
go home, or "return to base," as we say in flying. I liked San
Francisco, but I had never liked living there. No city is right for
everyone, and this one just wasn't right for me. My home-
sickness had never gone away—I cried myself to sleep almost
every night, it was so bad. By 2007, the year I decided to return
to Louisiana, I was quite literally counting the days until my
departure.

During the course of that last year, I took as many trips
back home as I could to visit my parents, and each time I took
the opportunity to go house hunting. On my third such
excursion, I found the perfect condo, an end unit on the top

floor of a small building located on one of the many outfall canals that lead to Lake Pontchartrain, at the northernmost end of the city. As such, it offered a view of both sunrise and sunset, plus a southern view of the downtown skyline. This was definitely it: my little lake Xanadu.

I closed on the condo about a month after I found it; about two months later, I was finally on my way back to New Orleans. Just like when I first moved to San Francisco, I was very nearly broke—the down payment on the condo and paying the movers sucked up almost every dime I had. But this time, I was so ecstatically happy that I couldn't care less about the money. It was okay if I couldn't afford some things for a while. I was going home.

I PICKED UP MY DAD FROM SAN FRANCISCO INTERNATIONAL on March 20, 2008. He would accompany me on my first cross-country trip in Orion, from San Francisco to New Orleans. After dreaming about this moment for years, it was really—finally!—going to happen. I was practically beside myself with excitement.

Earlier that week, a close friend who was also an instructor at my flying school had told me how envious he was of my upcoming trip. "So many small airplane pilots dream about doing something like that, but never actually do it," he said, wistful. "Even I've never flown that far in a small plane!"

His words got me even more amped up than I already was. I knew this would be a trip to remember.

When I'd decided to fly my plane home, I had promised myself two things: First, I would fly only in VMC (visual meteorological conditions)—in other words, I would avoid flying through clouds or fog or anything that might obscure visual references for the flight. Second, I would fly only during daylight hours. You always have to plan for the absolute worst crisis—an engine failure—and for me that meant not flying in IMC (instrument meteorological conditions) or at night. If your only engine quits, you want to be able to see the ground so you can pick the best and safest landing spot. I had also made sure to file a flight plan—another thing you do in case of a crash, so emergency rescue services know where to look for you based on the time you took off—from San Carlos (KSQL) to Blythe, California (KBLH), our first fuel stop, near the Arizona border.

We were all set to depart San Francisco on Good Friday. I'd hardly slept at all the night before from my excitement, so I felt pretty damn lousy, but I was too excited to care. And the three burly Russian movers I'd hired had showed up at 7:45 a.m.—fifteen minutes early—and were making excellent progress. *At this rate*, I thought, *we'll make it to at least New Mexico before nightfall!* But when they were done hauling out my already-packed boxes and started to pack the more delicate stuff—glasses, plates, and electronics—they slowed down considerably. With each passing minute, I amended our destination for the night in my head.

When planning long trips in a small plane, there are too many factors to consider to carve your overnight stops in stone. One of these factors is weather, such as winds aloft (which can be very different from surface winds) and storms. Winds aloft can either advance your progress, as with a tailwind, or hinder it, as with a headwind, and can mean the difference of taking away or adding an hour or more from what should normally be a four-hour trip. A storm can force you to go way off course, if you can get around it, or even force you to land someplace unplanned if you can't. Flying Orion, I didn't have the luxury of climbing over most weather like airliners do. So it would be pointless to try to pick today's destination and make a hotel reservation. That would have to be done on the fly (no pun intended, of course).

The movers didn't leave until 1 p.m. I had been hoping to be wheels up in the plane by then *at the latest*. I had at least been able to get in a short nap while they were packing. It was tough to sleep on the hard floor (my couch and bed were already in the truck) and with all the noise they were making, but I was tired enough that I'd managed to doze off for a bit.

We finally took off at 2 p.m. We started out at 7,500 feet, then climbed up to 11,500 feet for a short time when we took a mountain pass near Palm Springs—the San Bernardino Mountains to the north and the Santa Rosa Mountains to the south—before dropping back down to 7,500 feet. Even with my nap, I still hadn't gotten enough sleep, so the unpressurized elevation started to give me a headache pretty quickly. But the scenery was beautiful. Every peak over 7,000 feet was capped with snow, a sight that was still very alien to this Southern girl. My dad was just as taken with them as I was: he took some pictures with his iPhone and sent them to my mom.

We landed around 5:20 p.m. at Blythe, which the Airport/Facilities Directory (AFD), the book pilots use to find information about airports, had said had fuel. I taxied Orion to the ramp and parked near the fuel tank.

No one seemed to be around. I hopped down from the plane and walked over to the pump, credit card in hand. *Where do I pay?* I made a full circle around the tank, but couldn't find a place to swipe my card. *Crap!* This was not good. If we couldn't fuel up here, we'd either have to backtrack, something I really didn't want to do, or we'd have to go way off course to find another airport with fuel. Many places in the United States have small airports aplenty, but California's southern desert is not one of those places. And who knew if the same thing would happen at another airport? I had enough fuel to get us to one more place, but if we landed at the next place and couldn't fuel up there, we'd be stuck.

I looked up the contact number for the airport on my dad's iPhone and called it. No answer. Not a surprise, since it was now past 5:30 p.m. on a Friday.

"I'm going to go check out the pilot's lounge," I called to my dad, already walking toward it. "Maybe there's another number we can call!"

As I approached the lounge, I spotted a faded piece of paper taped to the window. *Bingo!* There it was: an after-hours number to call for fuel, with the name "Steve" written under it. An extra fee would apply, of course. Fine with me. I just wanted to get us out of there. I called the number.

"Hello?" a woman's voice answered.

"Um, is Steve there?" I asked. "I'm at the airport, and I need fuel."

She sighed. "Okay. He'll be there in about fifteen minutes." She hung up before I could respond.

While we waited, I calculated how long it would take us to get to Phoenix and started calling hotels near the small airports there to make sure they would come pick us up. I'd never flown someplace before and had a hotel within a few miles refuse to pick me up, but there's always a first time for everything, and I didn't want to risk getting stuck on the tarmac. Two hotels near the first airport I settled on refused to come pick us up, even though one was less than a mile away. There was also no taxi service—part of the joy of flying into small towns. So I looked up the next closest airport, in Goodyear, Arizona (KGYR), and the lady at a hotel I called nearby said we could get a cab. SOLD!

Day 1 of the trip, and I was already about to break Rule No. 2, "no flying after sunset." *Well, that didn't take long,* I thought. But you know what they say about rules.

Steve showed up while I was still on the phone calling hotels. He was a pretty big guy (I'm being kind), and he took his time walking over to the fuel tank. As I observed his glacial pace, I thought of the cartoons where the action cuts to a screen saying "Hours Later," and yet nothing has moved. This felt even more appropriate when Steve veered off, bypassed the tank, and busied himself with something else while my dad and I stood there baking in the desert heat, wondering if he'd ever come to fuel the plane.

When Steve finally approached the airplane, my dad gave him a broad grin.

"Hey, how's it going?" he asked.

Cue the crickets.

Figuring Steve hadn't heard him, my dad asked again: "How's it going?"

No response. The guy didn't even acknowledge our presence. Here we were, about to spend $250 on fuel and pay him extra to come out there after hours, and he couldn't even exchange pleasantries?

I looked at my dad and rolled my eyes. Given how many bad experiences I'd had in California, this little exchange was a fitting goodbye. It was definitely time to go home.

THE SUN WAS SETTING AND AN ORANGE MOON WAS rising over the lights of Phoenix in the distance as we crossed over the border into Arizona after leaving Blythe. Ahhh, homeward bound! I felt better already.

Goodyear Airport is a single-runway towered airport. It was dark by the time we got there, so all the airport lights were on, the greens, reds, blues, and whites arranged in perfect rows—a beautiful sight.

The line guy approached Orion as soon as we taxied to the ramp.

"Hi there," he said to my dad. "How was the flight?" He clearly thought my dad was the pilot.

My dad and I looked at each other and rolled our eyes. He knew the drill; he knew he'd be approached as the pilot or instructor nine times out of ten at least.

"It was fine," he said, "but she's the pilot, so ask her."

I don't hold it against anyone when that happens; there are so few women pilots that it's generally a safe bet the guy is the pilot. I could get annoyed, but it doesn't feel worth it.

Sexism aside, we found that the airport had a nice FBO (fixed base operation, where you can get fuel and arrange for other services in a nice, air-conditioned office with a friendly staff and usually some kind of free junk food like popcorn and cookies), and they even had a crew car that, for $25, we could use until we left the next morning. A crew car is usually a really old, worn-out auto some small airports make available for the convenience of transient pilots as long as they agree to put gas in it before returning it. It's one of those great old "honor systems" that are so rare these days. But not all airports have one, or sometimes another pilot will have taken it before you get there, so you can't ever just assume you'll have ground transportation when you arrive—yet another of the many details of flying a small plane that make every trip unpredictable. We were happy to take the car in this case, though, and after getting directions to our hotel, we headed out in the junky little thing.

After a subpar meal at TGI Fridays, we headed back to our hotel and—after I toured the in-house Bible museum, still riding out the last of my post-flying adrenaline buzz—we crashed.

THE NEXT MORNING, AFTER WE ATE BREAKFAST AT THE hotel, I called a weather briefer to check out the meteorological situation. Severe clear—an aviation term for when there's hardly a speck of cloud in the sky—was the forecast for our whole route. The Trim God, the fictional supreme being of aviation I first read about in *Air Vagabonds*, was clearly blessing my trip home with perfect weather!

Over the next couple days, we made quick headway. Each time we arrived in the next sectional (an aviation map broken into sections of the country), I would gladly toss the last one in the backseat where my favorite stuffed animal, a Mardi Gras clown, smiled about our progress. Okay, so he's a Mardi Gras clown with a permanent smile glued on, but his smile sure looked a lot brighter to me on this trip! Arizona and New Mexico went by in a blur. I would have liked to spend more time in New Mexico—more time to take in its strange, beautiful landscape—but I was on a mission, my tunnel vision pointing straight at New Orleans.

In El Paso, Texas, we got just the kind of treatment I had come to expect at small airports by this point: upon walking into the small pilots' lounge, I was greeted by an ultra-friendly lady who offered to let us take their pickup truck, parked out front, to go get ourselves some lunch while her husband fueled up Orion. I was also excited to see that her husband was working on a T-28 Trojan—a big old radial-engine taildragger

Me with Orion in San Carlos, California,
soon after I bought him.

Our formation flight on the way back from the aviation
convention in Palm Springs, California.

My flying chariot on the way back to the Bay Area
from Palm Springs.

Oh! The sights you'll see! Ocean and mountains – some of the
beautiful scenery Orion took me to, taken from the ramp at the
Shelter Cove Airport in Northern California.

San Francisco on a rare sunny summer day!

Crossing over the Sierra Mountains on my trip home with Dad.
The change in scenery as we went East was striking!
It went from snow-capped mountains ...

...to absolutely barren moonscape-looking mountains.

More cool terrain – this time the island and welcoming runway
of South Bimini in the Bahamas.

I will never tire of the colors of the Bahamas!
Landfall at Andros.

Ahhhhhh. Isn't this the most inviting hammock you've ever
seen? At The Cove, Eleuthera.

More gorgeous scenery at The Cove, Eleuthera.

My beloved hometown of New Orleans showing the Greater
New Orleans bridge, downtown, the Superdome, and the
Mighty Mississippi.

My awesome home airport – New Orleans Lakefront Airport.
It's hard to miss since it sticks out into Lake Pontchartrain.

Aviation Mecca, aka Oshkosh, Wisconsin during the annual
Experiment Aircraft Association fly-in. All those white things
on the grass are airplanes. Taken from downwind for the green
dot on Runway 27.

A close up of downtown New Orleans taken from a happy
passenger during Women in Aviation Week
(photo by Olivia Brinich).

Me and Orion just being us.

with a closed cockpit in which pretty much every military pilot was trained to fly during the 1940s and 1950s. You never know what you'll see at a small airport!

Our other truly memorable experience during the trip was our stay at the Hangar Hotel, a cool hotel constructed in an actual hangar right at the airport in Fredericksburg, Texas. We arrived there at dusk on the final eve of our journey, and touched down in front of a balcony full of people enjoying the sunset—and my landing, which, thankfully, was a smooth one. As we parked Orion right in front of the hotel, I thought about getting out and taking a bow, and had a vision of the people on the balcony holding scorecards to rate my landing. (Luckily, I didn't know the people were there until after we landed. I'm sure if I'd known they were watching, my performance would have been terrible; it's almost guaranteed that when I'm flying around someone I want to impress, the landing will be one of my worst ever. Such is a pilot's life.)

We secured the airplane and went inside. What a great idea for a hotel! Whoever decorated the place had clearly had a really good time with the South Pacific/art deco theme. Every little detail went along with it: even the front-desk guy wore a pilot's uniform. Aviation decorations hung from the ceiling. Our room had a green army blanket with the Hangar Hotel logo on it, a telephone made to look like a rotary phone, and cute notecards printed with sayings such as "Urgent message from the front lines—please use these towels for makeup removal," and "Communiqué from intelligence—please contact the front desk if you need assistance." There was also an Officers' Club downstairs where a pianist was playing hits from the World War II era.

Our dinner that night was about what you'd expect in Texas. We went across the highway from our hotel to a place called the Cotton Gin—a fairly classy place—and as I scanned the menu, the exotic-sounding buffalo enchiladas on the menu caught my eye. *Hmm,* I thought, *I wonder what buffalo tastes like?* So I asked. According to the waitress, "It's somewhere between deer and antelope."

Oh, well, that clears it right up, doesn't it?

For the record, buffalo tastes pretty much the same as beef. But maybe beef is also somewhere between deer and antelope—hell if I know!

AFTER A DAMNED GOOD SUNDAY BREAKFAST THE NEXT day (I had grits—oh, it was so good to be back in the South!), we ordered two sandwiches for the road and got back in Orion for the last leg of our trip.

A small storm had been predicted when I checked the weather the night before, but it had never materialized, so the skies were clear all the way to New Orleans. In fact, as it happened, I never once had to change altitude for so much as a cloud in the entire course of our journey. That's nearly unheard of for such a long haul, this one almost 1,800 miles. I was so grateful I would have happily sacrificed a virgin to the Trim God if I could have found one. So many things were showing me that this trip was truly meant to be. (And it didn't hurt that the attitude of the people and the quality and prices of the food kept improving as we traveled farther South.)

We crossed into Louisiana as my dad snapped a picture of the Sabine River, carving its circuitous route along the border, and in no time we were talking to Baton Rouge approach—near home turf! We had to stop in Jennings (3R7) for fuel, and it was gusty as all hell—the landing there was a hard-fought one. But stressful as it was, I could barely contain my glee as we fueled up and prepared to take off again. I knew the next time I set the airplane up for a landing it would be at my home airport.

As we drew closer to our destination, I was told to change frequency and contact New Orleans approach control.

I changed to the frequency that the Baton Rouge controller gave me, keyed my microphone with a huge smile, and gave my tail number, altitude, and flight rules I was flying under.

"New Orleans Approach, good afternoon, Skyhawk five niner zero sierra papa, level three thousand five hundred, VFR."

"November five niner zero sierra papa, confirm destination Lakefront," the controller replied. They often ask you to confirm or say where you're going.

"Zero sierra papa, affirmative!" My heart swelled.

It was so comforting to hear a pilot with a Cajun accent talking to the controller. His accent meant I was home, and it was music to my ears!

Louis Armstrong International Airport, which I still call Moisant (its name until 2001), is the large, commercial service airport for New Orleans, though it is located in the suburb of Kenner. Its airport identifier, MSY, stands for Moisant Stock Yards, which occupied the space before it was an airport and was named for the family of John Moisant, an early aviation pioneer.

The New Orleans sectional showed an airspace corridor directly over MSY that went from 1,000 to 2,000 feet for traffic transitioning the airspace rather than landing. Before my trip, I had asked a friend in New Orleans how easy it was to get cleared through this corridor.

"It's almost a joke," he said. "They'll vector you right through MSY's bravo airspace."

Bravo airspace is the most restrictive of the different classes of controlled airspace. Usually you get a bravo clearance just a few minutes before you enter, but my friend was right: they cleared me through it when I was still fifteen minutes out, the easiest bravo clearance I've ever gotten. I had become used to the very complicated airspace around San Francisco and enduring a more difficult clearance, if I even got one at all. In this case, however, I was vectored just south, almost directly over MSY, so we got a great view of the huge runways. I took that piece of luck as another sign: the air traffic controllers were unknowingly welcoming me home!

Lakefront Airport, my destination, was the original airport serving New Orleans and hence has the more logical identifier NEW. It is only twelve nautical miles (NM) from Louis Armstrong Airport, and 12 NM doesn't take long when you're doing 120 knots. So in no time I was practically on top of the traffic pattern at Lakefront, and I was starting to sweat it because I hadn't gotten a hand-off from New Orleans approach control to Lakefront tower yet.

I decided not to wait for the hand-off any longer: "Zero Sierra Papa is landing Lakefront," I said into the radio. "Frequency change, please?" I quickly switched the radio frequency to the Lakefront control tower and spat out, "Lakefront Airport, Skyhawk five niner zero sierra papa, West End, landing, whiskey" as quickly as I could so I could get permission to land there before I entered their airspace without a clearance. West End is a big street in that part of town, and you always let the controller know where you are so he can slot you in the right order to land if there is more than one airplane coming in or out. "Whiskey" was the phonetic alphabet identifier of the hourly weather update at the airport; by including it in my communication to the controller, I was telling him that I had the current local weather and wind report. The tower controller responded immediately, to my relief, and cleared me to land on 36 left, a runway a whopping 6,879 feet long.

It had been a little over four years since I last landed a plane (with a lot of help back then, since it was during my first few lessons with Bart) at Lakefront Airport. Even though the airport itself had changed very little, it looked so different to me now. It looked like a big welcome home, as if the long runway I was approaching was waving me in, ready to envelop my airplane in its immensity.

It was very windy, but the wind was blowing straight down the runway in our direction. This meant I'd need a little more throttle than usual, so I advanced the throttle slightly as I watched my approach angle and airspeed, and kept my right hand on it in case the wind got stronger or weaker, something you can never see before it happens but have to react to quickly when on final approach. I took a deep breath as we crossed just over the runway numbers, noting them carefully since I knew I'd be seeing them often from now on—this was my new home airport, after all. I slowly closed the throttle as the airplane settled in ground effect and then gently touched down. I landed using hardly any runway at all, and turned off at the first taxiway as my dad patted me on the back. It was like it was meant to be.

I teared up a little as we taxied, though I tried to hide it. We were home.

IT WAS GRATIFYING TO SEE HOW MUCH MY DAD HAD enjoyed the trip—a fact that became clear when my mom picked us up and brought us back to their house for Easter dinner with my brother and his family, and my dad couldn't stop talking about it. During dinner, I'd be talking to one person about some aspect of the journey, and I'd hear Dad talking to someone else about another detail.

I was just telling my brother and his wife, "...and then she said, 'Buffalo is somewhere between deer and antelope,' and I looked at Dad, and we both laughed since we had no idea what those tasted like either!"

When their laughter calmed down, I heard my dad, turned the other way, telling my parents-in-law another story about Texas: "There was *actual* tumbleweed that had blown up to the plane and was sitting against the landing gear," he said, chuckling. "And the accents of the air traffic controllers—well, let's just say it was perfectly obvious when we crossed into Texas, and when we crossed out of it."

I had, according to that instructor from my California flying club, just completed a flight that few small airplane pilots actually ever do. I felt like I had just graduated to another level of pilot, even though I had no new rating or endorsement in my logbook. The trip also showed me that I could, indeed, go quite far even though my plane wasn't ever the biggest or fastest on the ramp.

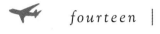 *fourteen* | BAHAMAS, BABY!

"A good traveler has no fixed plans and is not intent on arriving."
—LAO TZU

THE WINTER OF 2009 STARTED VERY EARLY AND was unusually harsh. Normally we only get one or two hard freezes in New Orleans each winter, but that year we had multiple hard freezes, plus a number of light freezes, too. Any time the temperature drops below 70 degrees in Louisiana, I start daydreaming of latitudes south. I had also been home in New Orleans for almost two years now, and had barely taken any vacation except a rare day here and there—and since I was still working for the same company that I'd worked for in San Francisco, I had accrued a ton of unused vacation days. So it seemed like fate when I read—bundled up but still shivering at my computer—an article written by another pilot about flying his small plane to the Bahamas.

I was already scheming how to do my own Bahamas trip before I finished the article. But flying over water in a single-engine airplane can be risky. I decided I should take someone along. It would be nice to have some company, and someone to share expenses with, anyway.

I called Nick, the same pilot friend who had set me up with Wingman.

During my time in California, we had talked about going on a long trip together in the plane, so when I said, "I want to fly my plane to the Bahamas for two weeks but want company and someone to share the expenses. You in?" he jumped at the chance and said, "YES!" immediately, almost before I could get the question out.

Nick and I made it as far as talking about all the extra safety items we would take in the airplane. But then, about three weeks before the trip, he got laid off and had to start a new job.

"Sorry, Erin," he said when he called. "I just don't have the vacation time anymore, and I definitely can't take time off in my first month."

I was bummed out, but I tried to put a positive spin on things: *It'll be easier to immerse myself with the locals and to get a sense of what life is really like in the islands if I go alone*, I thought. *Maybe it's for the best*.

I started preparing for my trip in earnest now. I had already ordered a specialty over-water emergency kit in case I had to ditch the plane in the big pond; now I bought a SPOT Messenger personal-locator beacon (PLB) with a button that I could press to ping my parents (and anyone else I set up in the system) with a text each time I landed to let them know I was okay, along with a link that would show them where I was. I hoped that text and map would keep my parents from worrying too much during the hours it sometimes took me to get to a place I could call them when I was traveling. The SPOT also has a button you can press to contact local emergency services and anyone else whose information you enter in the system if you have some sort of emergency, which was reassuring.

Nick, always a cautious pilot, also insisted that I get a life raft, but I couldn't afford one—even the one-person model had a $1,000-plus price tag. I did have Coast Guard–approved life jackets, though. I figured between those and the PLB, I'd be okay. I did, however, pack some MREs (military meals ready to eat)—left over from when the police handed them out after Hurricane Katrina—plus some snacks, in case I got stuck someplace for a while. Now I felt sufficiently covered in the event that anything bad happened. I was ready to fly.

I STARTED TO TENSE UP A FEW DAYS BEFORE MY scheduled departure in early December when every local newscast began to report that we could expect mixed precipitation (sleet/snow/rain) Friday night into Saturday morning. Apparently someone had forgotten that this was New Orleans and that type of weather didn't happen here. Then again, it shouldn't have come as a surprise: ever since I'd moved back, every time I'd scheduled my airplane, the weather had tanked. It's the strongest correlation I've seen with anything having to do with the weather. I often felt like I was paying for the perfect weather I'd had on the flight home. If there was one thing I missed about California, it was the almost-always-perfect flying conditions, a stark contrast to the often volatile weather of the South. Since I'd scheduled this trip to the Bahamas about two months ago, I figured, the universe had had a lot of time to plan for sending some really lousy weather my way.

On Thursday, the forecast improved a tiny bit: the weather was now just supposed to be stormy Friday night and then clear out Saturday morning, to be followed by a high-level high-pressure system. A high-pressure system is what every pilot hopes for: it means clear weather. On Friday night, I attended my condo building holiday party—at which the second stranger in one week offered to come with me—but left early to call a weather briefer and check on the forecast again. Not as good as it had sounded before. I talked to the briefer for about a half hour to get the full picture, and got off the phone deflated. It looked like my long-dreamed-about vacation was going to have to wait out the bad weather.

Still, I decided to be optimistic: I filed the customs forms to fly out the next morning. I would refuel in Cross City, Florida, then fly over Orlando, leave the coast at Boca Raton, and fly into Freeport International Airport, Grand Bahama. I figured I'd start the island hopping in the northern islands and then take a clockwise route south and then back up to Florida. And I had a whole two weeks to island hop to my heart's content!

Feeling more hopeful now, I called my parents and asked them to pick me up at 8:00 a.m. the next day to bring me to Lakefront Airport.

THE NEXT MORNING, I WOKE UP AT SEVEN THIRTY (luxuriously late for me—I usually wake up at five thirty for work) and checked the weather online. Not great.

Guess I'm not going anywhere anytime soon. I decided to go for a five-mile run and asked my parents to stand by. I had planned to be on my way to the Bahamas already by this point, so everything was packed—I had nothing else to do. Never mind that the temperature was 34 degrees with a wind chill factor in the high twenties; I figured a run was a good way to take my mind off of not being on my way to warmer weather. I bundled up (I even put on my vintage leather flying helmet, the only hat I had that covers my ears), and hit the trail.

Despite all the layers I had put on, it was miserably cold on my run. But at least the struggle of physical exertion was mellowing me out. Of course, tons of variables were running through my head: weather, when I could leave, when would that put me at my planned stops, when would I ever get to the Bahamas, would the weather be this bad coming back ... I'd love to be able to shut of my brain sometimes so I'm not fretting over a million details, but when it's just me and the sound of my breath, it's hard for my mind to not wander to the task at hand.

Toward the end of my run, the weather was starting to clear up in New Orleans. The system was headed east, though, so I'd either have to wait for it to clear along my route or fly behind it at 20 mph. Some people say my plane is slow, but it ain't that slow! I checked the weather yet again when I got back, and it sounded like I could leave around noon and get to Gainesville, Florida, just when Gainesville would be getting clear enough to fly VFR. I asked my parents to come by at noon for me. *This is it!* I thought, getting excited again.

When we finally got to the airport, I started the first few items on my preflight inspection checklist, shivering as I went. Lakefront Airport is right on Lake Pontchartrain, and when the wind is out of the north, it can get damned frigid. With icy, shaking fingers, I turned on the plane's master power switch, lowered the flaps, turned on all the navigation lights, and checked the fuel gauges. Then I walked to the end of the pilot's-side wing and ducked to check the beacon flashing at the top of the tail and the port-side navigation light and strobe. Next I walked toward the front to check the landing and taxi lights—and stopped. They weren't on.

"I may cry in a minute," I mumbled to my parents.

What was going on? I walked back to the cockpit to see if the switches for those lights were on and then walked back out.

The lights were still off. I cycled the switches. Still off. Every-thing else was working, but not these lights. *No way. NO WAY!* I needed a landing light to legally fly. I was going to be grounded until I got them working again—and it was Saturday. What mechanic works on a Saturday? That meant I'd be stuck in town until Monday, and I already knew that the weather pre-dicted for the beginning of the week would keep me in New Orleans still longer than that.

All these thoughts were going through my head as I locked the plane door and turned to face my parents.

"I have to go back to the FBO to see if I can find anyone who can fix the lights," I grumbled.

My parents both started asking questions:

"What would cause both the landing and taxi light to go out?"

"When were they were last replaced?"

"What will we do if no one's here that can fix them?"

"I don't know, okay?" I said, getting short-tempered. They were asking perfectly good questions, but I was starting to wonder what else could go wrong to keep me from taking this vacation, and it was making me snippy.

My parents followed me to the FBO, where the receptionist started making calls on my behalf to all the maintenance people who worked on the field, even ones who worked at competing FBOs. She was getting a lot of voicemails. But she got a hold of some people. One airplane owner said he'd call his mechanic. One of the flight school instructors said he'd call a mechanic friend in Mississippi. Nothing came of either lead. After she'd been calling for a while, my dad and I walked back out to see if maybe the problem was a fluke. It didn't seem to be. But just as my dad started to unscrew the plastic cover to the lights (both the landing and taxi lights sit next to each other on the leading edge of the pilot's-side wing), the receptionist called me to say she'd reached a maintenance guy who said he'd come out. Bless the Trim God!

I taxied my plane to the nearby maintenance hangar to wait for the mechanic to show—which, thankfully, didn't take long. He was very friendly for someone who had been called in to work on his day off, too. It turned out that both bulbs had burned out; odd that it happened at the same time, usually that doesn't happen.

"Can you think of any reason that would have happened?" I asked.

"Hm." He scratched his head. "The only explanation I can think of is that someone might've landed the plane hard enough to knock them out."

Ouch. I didn't like the sound of that. Not because I thought I was the one who did it—my landings hadn't been that rough in years once I got the hang of it. But just like I had in California, I made Orion available for rent at a local flying school to (slightly) offset the blood-curdling costs of owning and maintaining it. I hated the idea that those student pilots were beating the crap out of my pride and joy.

I taxied back to drop off my dad and say goodbye to my mom, who had wisely chosen to wait with the receptionist at the flight school rather than freeze outside.

Our goodbye was more abrupt than I wanted it to be—a quick exchange of goodbyes and I love yous, as if I were leaving their house after dinner rather than heading out into the unknown with my plane. I hated that. I wanted to tell them how much they meant to me, to thank them for all they did for me, but I couldn't seem to find the words. I'd considered leaving them a note expressing all the things I never managed to verbalize—but if I ever mentioned even the *possibility* of dying in flight, I don't think my mom could take it. Still, I knew that anytime I went up in my plane, something bad could happen. I hoped that if something were to happen, my training would allow me to manage it, but there are some crises that a pilot can't fix. I worried sometimes that something might happen to me without me having said all the things I wanted to say to them.

My parents were already getting into the car when my mom paused. "Oh!" she said. "Almost forgot." She leaned into the backseat then hurried back over to me. "Here," she said, handing me a brown paper sack. "So you don't starve."

My mom had made me a bag lunch. I couldn't help but smile and chill out a bit. What great motherly foresight. She knew I had been getting more and more wound up about the bad weather and not being able to leave. This was her way of trying to make me feel better. And it was working.

The flight was uneventful, except for the fact that I had to hand-fly the airplane since Otto (what I and most other pilots call their autopilot) wasn't working. I tried it. Twice. The first time, it made a 90-degree turn to the right and then made a 180-degree turn to the left. The course was in the middle. I disconnected it, then reconnected it and tried to engage it using a different navigation mode, but it wouldn't quite sync up; all it would do was parallel my course. Since I was threading through numerous patches of restricted airspace, I was uncomfortable with this, so I disconnected it again. I landed at Tallahassee, Florida, about twenty minutes after sunset. So much for making the Bahamas in one day.

There was one highlight to my flight, however: in true mom fashion, my mom had stuck a sticky note onto a moist towelette inside the bag lunch she made me that said, "Enjoy Relax Have Fun Love Ya!!" Though the sticky note got a little wet with juice from the ham sandwich, I saved it as a reminder. Because she was right—I did need to learn to enjoy, relax, and have fun. That's what vacations and flying are all about; stressing about the weather, which I couldn't change, was pointless. I promised myself I would try harder to lighten up and let go for the rest of my trip.

I WOKE UP THE NEXT DAY IN A BETTER MOOD, HOPING that I would finally get to the Bahamas and out of the cold weather that day. I called a weather briefer.

"It's VFR all the way to Palm Beach, but there's a stationary low over Grand Bahama and low cloud ceilings all day," he told me.

VFR stands for visual flight rules. It means (in the United States, anyway) that the pilot must have at least three miles of visibility, and that the cloud ceiling—the lowest layer of clouds that covers more than half of the sky—must be at least 1,000 feet high in order to legally fly without an IFR (instrument flight rules) flight plan and clearance. IFR means the weather is such that visibility and cloud ceiling are less than VFR, so the pilot must fly the plane mostly or even solely by reference to the instruments rather than observing what is outside. I had an instrument rating, enabling me to fly in IMC (instrument meteorological conditions) if I wished, but it's more risky to do that in an unfamiliar area—not a boundary I wanted to test on this trip. So I decided to land in Lantana, Florida, near Palm Beach, and see what the weather was doing by then.

Once in the air, it appeared that Otto was still on vacation —and not the same vacation I was on. I tried it again on two different modes, but neither mode worked. It seemed as if my autopilot "knew" what my course was, but it wouldn't capture the course—it just kept zigzagging around it in huge waves. So in the end, I had to hand-fly Orion again the whole rest of the way, an inconvenience for such a long flight.

I felt myself tensing up over Otto's failure to cooperate—*I could really use a minute to sit back and stretch*, I thought. But then I reminded myself that I was supposed to enjoy this vacation, no matter what. I consciously made the decision to relax. *Oh well*, I told myself. *This is why I fly, right? Adventure!*

AS IT TURNED OUT, THE WEATHER HEAVILY INFLUENCED all of my flights in the Bahamas. So it's worth talking a bit more about some aviation weather points.

As I mentioned a moment ago, there are two general types of flight rules: visual (VFR) and instrument (IFR). VFR varies a bit between countries and different types of airspace, but generally means that the pilot has at least a 1,000-foot cloud ceiling and is at least 500 feet below, 1,000 feet above, and 2,000 feet vertical from any cloud. IFR comes into play when the pilot is flying the airplane solely by reference to the instruments, as when she's in a cloud and can't see outside. Implementing IFR is also not as simple as flying through a cloud when you want or need to, however. Before you can do that, you must notify air traffic control and get a special IFR flight plan clearance. This is possible to obtain in the air, say when you start off a flight VFR but then encounter cloudiness along the way, but it's easier to plan a whole flight IFR so you can pick up what is sometimes a lengthy clearance on the ground and not on the fly.

Even though I have an instrument rating and can legally fly IFR, I always prefer to fly VFR, primarily because the main reason I fly is to enjoy the view. To me, flying IFR is like going to New York City just to see the Statue of Liberty and then not being able to see her when you get there because she's totally covered in fog. I fly IFR if I absolutely have to get somewhere, but on pleasure trips, like this vacation, I *definitely* want to be able to see! But my preference for flying VFR isn't just about aesthetics—it's also very much about safety. I need to be able to pick a safe place to land if my engine quits, and I've heard too many stories of pilots losing an engine while in IMC and making an unsafe landing or worse because they only broke out of the clouds a few hundred feet over the ground, not enough time to find a good spot and set up a glide to get there safely.

There's a lot to consider when you're planning a flight and trying to determine whether it will be IFR or VFR. Clouds, for example, are tricky things. Every cloud layer has four divisions, from clearest to cloudiest: few, scattered, broken, and overcast. "Few" means that the clouds cover zero to two-eighths of the sky; scattered means they cover three- to four-eighths of the sky; broken means five- to seven-eighths of the sky; and overcast means that clouds cover the entire sky. A cloud ceiling, as defined for VFR flight, is the lowest broken or overcast cloud layer. So if it's a particularly dreary day with overcast clouds at eight hundred feet, you are in IFR conditions. But sometimes there is just one cloud layer and as soon as you climb through it, it's a nice sunny day on top. Nothing is ever certain when flying a small plane!

My unwillingness to fly IFR means I sometimes have to postpone flights, but I'm okay with that. I'll take safety—and gorgeous views—over the alternative.

IT WAS HIGH OVERCAST UNTIL JUST BEFORE ORLANDO. There, the cloud ceiling came way down. I could see a layer up ahead that looked like it was at my altitude (3,500 feet), but you can't fly below 3,000 feet when you're over Disney World; I guess Mickey Mouse and company don't like the sound of airplanes overhead. After a lot of runaround from the air traffic controller—he vectored me around the Palm Beach International airspace and told me to expect to fly a mile out over the ocean at 1,000 feet and then turn south, but then got so busy with traffic that he was talking as fast as he could and still couldn't talk fast enough, so I ended up being way farther out over the water than I expected—I was finally allowed to turn back in towards land and contact the UNICOM (a kind of a do-it-yourself tower-controller system that many small airports that can't afford a tower use).

Lantana is a three-runway airport, its runways arranged in a triangle pattern. After flying into it, I can't understand how a place that busy gets by without a control tower. Normally, if an airport has enough traffic, the associated fuel taxes and airport fees alone are enough to support a tower, and this was one busy airport. One guy who was flying south along the shoreline and not talking on the radio almost ran straight into me—he had to turn away at the last minute. I saw him coming, so I would have been able to maneuver around him if I had to, but it would have been nice if he had been talking to us on the CTAF (common traffic advisory frequency) and looking out the goddamned window.

When the guy finally got on the radio and reported his position, I couldn't resist calling him out: "Were you the one who almost hit me?" I asked.

"Yeah," he mumbled. No apology. Just a "yeah."

Nice. So far, this was not the relaxing vacation I had hoped for.

I landed in a headwind so strong that I must have touched down at about 20 knots versus my normal approach speed of 65 knots on final, which slows down to about 50–60 knots by the time I touch down. But with a headwind that strong, it makes it easy to make a short landing, as if I were landing on an aircraft carrier. Anywhere else, wind like that would scare off many pilots, but given how full of traffic the pattern was there, I guessed high winds must be normal in that area. For my part, I was glad to be on the ground and out of the mess of airplanes buzzing around.

The wind whistled in my ears as I tied Orion down, whipping dirt into my mouth, ears, and anywhere else that presented itself (and some places that didn't). I finished up as quickly as possible, then made a beeline into the FBO and found a very friendly staff who offered me the crew car for the night. Sweet! Now I'd be able to get around.

Crew cars are notorious for being really crappy. This one was dented, all scratched up, smelled of beef jerky, and even had dirty socks wadded up in a ball on the backseat. I couldn't help but smile. Now this trip was beginning to look more like the adventure I had hoped for! I headed for my hotel while I tried to ignore the smell of beef jerky mixed with dirty socks.

After cruising A1A for a while, I called it an early night. I went to bed excited that I was now in the land that Jimmy Buffett, a fellow pilot, sings about. In the morning, I hoped, it would be Grand Bahama or bust!

THE NATION OF THE BAHAMAS COMPRISES MORE THAN 3,000 islands, with a total land area of 5,382 square miles. It sits southeast of Florida, and north of Cuba and the island of Hispaniola (the Dominican Republic and Haiti). The two Bahamian islands closest to the United States are Grand Bahama (the northernmost island with an airport, where I was planning to start my adventure but not stay for long, because it seemed too touristy for my taste) and Bimini, both of which are 55 to 60 miles off Florida. Since I was taking a risk flying a single-engine plane over open water, I wanted to start on one of those islands and then work my way south to the outer islands, away from the touristy islands of Nassau and Grand Bahama. I was also limited in where I could make my entry because not every island has international customs clearance.

I took a morning run by a lagoon in a beautiful park when I woke up that day in Lantana, and the weather wasn't looking good. Pilots develop a knack for estimating cloud height (because many of our flights depend on it), so of course I was checking that out as I ran, and the sky was fairly clear where I was—maybe a few to scattered clouds at about 2,500 feet, nothing too ominous—but I could see the towering cumulonimbi to the east, where I was hoping to go. I had already checked the weather online, and it was looking equally bleak. So I was trying to enjoy myself at the park. *Travel is not always about the destination*, I reminded myself. *Getting there and back is part of the adventure.*

I was just starting to relax when I noticed a rather alarming sign: "WARNING: ALLIGATORS MAY BE PRESENT." I picked up speed. So much for a relaxing run!

After (optimistically) checking out of my hotel and heading back to the airport, I sat down and called Flight Service. A very helpful briefer with a thick Latino accent answered, and we discussed the weather situation at length—though it took even longer than usual due to the language barrier (mostly me having a hard time understanding him).

"The stationary front is still parked over Grand Bahama," he told me, "but it is mostly clear south of it."

It occurred to me that maybe I should reverse the trip I had originally planned—fly to Bimini first, then island hop counterclockwise back to Florida. I ran the idea by my new friend. "What do you think?" I asked.

"There is no weather reporting station at Bimini," he said. "But I can look up Nassau. That's the closest station."

That was still a good 124 miles away, so not extremely useful to me other than for a general picture of conditions, but it was better than nothing. "That would be great," I said. "How does it look?"

"Nassau is reporting few clouds at 2,500 feet," he said.

Time to go while the weather was still flyable! I thanked him profusely, hung up, and headed straight for my plane.

Naturally, once I got airborne, conditions were mostly cloudy over Florida, with the clouds at different altitudes. I was originally assigned 2,500 feet, but I had to ask for higher to steer clear of those clouds, then went to 3,500 feet and in a few minutes had to ask to go higher again, traveling up to 4,500 feet, where I stayed marginally VFR. I needed to open my ICAO flight plan (international flight plan, which is required when crossing the U.S. Air Defense Identification Zone, or ADIZ) on another radio frequency with Miami Center, but the air traffic controller on my assigned frequency was talking a mile a minute and I couldn't get a word in. This was some of the busiest airspace I'd ever been in, rivaling the Bay Area's heavy traffic.

The departure controllers were having me change radio frequencies like mad, normally something you only do once every thirty minutes or so at my speed of entering and exiting each control area, and maybe even less frequently than that, as you fly into a different airspace region. One controller even changed me to another frequency just seconds after I checked in with him. I was fiddling with the tuner so quickly that my fingers were practically smoking.

When does the relaxing part of this vacation start? I wondered. I hoped Bimini was the answer.

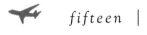 *fifteen* | BIMINI,
FINALLY!

*"For my part, I travel not to go anywhere, but to go.
I travel for travel's sake. The great affair is to move."*
—ROBERT LOUIS STEVENSON

HE WATER WAS A GORGEOUS CERULEAN BLUE
as I set my course for Bimini. I had finally been given
the okay to turn east and head out over the water.
Unfortunately, I was still dealing with clouds, so I couldn't
really admire the beauty as much as I wanted to. Rather than
the reported few clouds at 2,500 feet, the sky was scattered at
1,000 feet, and I was now at 1,500 feet, flying over the cloud
layer. And, of course, right where the island should be in the
distance, there was a mass of clouds instead.

Filing a flight plan is not usually a requirement when flying
VFR, but since I had to cross the US Air Defense Identification
Zone (ADIZ) to get to Bimini, I had been required to file a flight
plan before leaving Florida. And once you "open" or activate
your flight plan, you have to be sure to close it upon arrival,
either by phone or by talking to an air traffic controller, within
thirty minutes of your scheduled arrival time, or they send
search and rescue for you. Since I wasn't sure what the phone

situation would be on Bimini, I decided to close my flight plan from the air, before I landed.

About 10 miles out from Bimini, I had to descend to avoid flying into a cloud layer right at 1,500 feet. Once I leveled off, I tried calling Miami Center on four different frequencies, to no avail—not a huge surprise, since airplane radios operate only on "line of sight" (meaning if the radio can't "see" the transmission tower, you won't be able to reach anyone) and I was down at 700 feet to stay VFR. Down there, I was below reception altitude. *Crap.* I still had the option of calling Miami once I landed in Bimini and canceling my flight plan that way, but I wasn't sure if my cell phone would have reception or if there even would be a pay phone I could use. I sighed. *Guess I'll find out soon enough.*

Meanwhile, the water had turned from the deep turquoise it had been closer to Florida to the palest of pale blues. The water was so clear, I felt like I was flying over a huge swimming pool. The land itself was still obscured by clouds, but the lighter shades of blue told me I was nearing the island. I snapped picture after picture of only water below me and only sky ahead of me, no land was in sight, grinning like a fool. Many single-engine pilots never venture out over open water, and here I was, going it alone. *Now this is what I came here for.*

BIMINI IS MADE UP OF TWO MAIN ISLANDS, SOUTH Bimini and North Bimini, and it sits on the top of a landmass that plunges thousands of feet underwater and into the Gulf Stream. Its original inhabitants, the Taino Indians, later called Lucayans, are estimated to have moved to the Bahamas from Cuba and Hispaniola around the eleventh century, and to have numbered more than 30,000 when Columbus first arrived in 1492. Historians believe his first landfall in the "new world" was on San Salvador in the southeastern Bahamas. Unfortunately for the Lucayans, the arrival of Columbus, the Europeans, their diseases, and their use of slavery wiped out the culture.

There are two theories about the word "Bimini": some believe that it came from the language of the Lucayans and means "two islands"; others believe the word is derived from the Taino words of "bibi" (mother) and "mini" (waters). The place itself has many claims to fame: it served as a base for "wreakers," thieves who preyed on the numerous shipwrecks in the area during the nineteenth century; its islands were the setting of many fishing scenes in Hemingway's *The Old Man and the Sea* and *Islands in the Stream* (he lived on North Bimini during the fishing seasons in the 1930s); and rumrunners used it as a stopover during the Prohibition era. Quite the colorful and checkered history! I had read up on all this before leaving the US, so I was excited to see the place for myself.

When Bimini finally came into view, it looked like an out-of-the-way island lover's paradise. Surrounded by a sea of crystal clear, light blue water, South Bimini island, where the airport is located, was completely covered in lush green foliage, save for what looked like a big slice cut in the middle of the island—the runway.

I flipped to the Bimini traffic frequency and reported my position: "Bimini traffic, Skyhawk five niner zero sierra papa is ten miles to the west and will be landing full stop, Bimini." I had been listening to the frequency for a while and knew there was no one else in the traffic pattern, but protocol is protocol.

Immediately after I radioed in, another pilot got on the same frequency—but I couldn't understand a word he was saying, except that he was calling his position as downwind to land, which was where I was about to be. All non-towered airports (there were only two in the Bahamas that were towered) in the Bahamas use the same frequency, so I figured he was probably at another airport, but for the life of me, I couldn't make out which airport he was reporting.

"Say again?" I asked.

He did, and I still couldn't understand.

"Say again which airport?" I asked again.

Another stream of unintelligible gibberish.

I really did not want to end my vacation before it began by crashing into another airplane. Finally I just asked, a little panic in my voice, "Are you at Bimini?"

He said, "No, another island."

That I understood. Thank God.

When airports do not have a control tower with air traffic controllers to give landing and takeoff clearances, you're supposed to report your position repeatedly as you get closer to the airport, essentially to "claim" your spot in the traffic pattern and then claim the runway when you are ready to land. When more than one plane is in the traffic pattern, self-reporting allows you to space yourself a safe distance from any other planes— and when you say you are on final approach for the runway, no one else is supposed to land until you report that you are clear of the runway. It's nice to have an air traffic controller running the show, but self-reporting does the job pretty well, as long as everyone's doing what they're supposed to do.

"Bimini traffic, Skyhawk five niner zero sierra papa on left downwind, landing to the east, full stop, Bimini," I said. What to say on the radio is often something that evokes great fear in student pilots. You don't want to say something wrong or stupid when others are listening. But once you get the hang of what to say and when to say it, like all those seemingly random gauges on the instrument panel that once baffled me, it becomes second nature to report your position when approaching airports and when you're in the traffic pattern. Sometimes you know you're talking to yourself when there's no one else around, and sometimes an airport is so busy you can hardly get a word in. But even when no one else is around, like there in Bimini, you still do it, just in case. You never know when someone else might enter the area unexpectedly.

Unlike most runways in more populated areas, the runway at Bimini was not marked with numbers, so I couldn't say the number of the runway I was landing on. A runway number denotes compass direction; you just add a zero to the end of the number. So runway 27, for example, is oriented at 270 degrees. I had never landed on a runway before that was not numbered, but I remembered that I'd heard pilots, when they had forgotten the runway number, simply say what direction they would be landing. So I finally just said, "Landing to the east."

I realized there were no taxiways once I was on the ground, so I just "back taxied" (made a U-turn while still on the runway) down the runway to the other end and parked near a small house perched at the end of the tarmac. WELCOME TO BIMINI, a sign in the window read. *I guess this is the customs office?* It was more shack than office, but I didn't see anything else that might be it.

I was really fretting about not having been able to close my flight plan from the air; I really did not want them sending search and rescue out after me. I needed to get myself to a phone, ASAP. I jumped out of Orion, locked him up, and ran into the customs office.

"Do you have a phone I can use?" I asked the customs agent, a little breathless from my sprint inside.

With an indifferent expression on his face, the customs agent wordlessly pointed me to a phone.

Phew, I thought—but then I picked up the phone, and there was so much static on the line it made me wince. *Oh well, better than nothing.*

I dialed Miami Center, and could only make out a few words coming from the person on the other end. That was fine: I didn't need to be able to hear them. I just needed them to be able to hear *me* well enough to get my tail number, that I wanted to close my flight plan, and that I was on the ground in Bimini.

Message communicated by yelling into the phone, I hung up the phone, rubbed my poor, abused ear (as if that would make it feel better after all that painful static), and I turned around to find that every last person in the room was staring at me. Having somewhat already introduced myself as the overbearing American, I smiled and said shyly, "Uh ... hi. How y'all doin'?" I got no response, so I shuffled my way back over to the desk to deal with customs.

The customs agent asked the basic question first: "Where are you coming from?" That one went off without a hitch. Then it got more complicated—he asked where else I was going, how long I was going to be in Bimini, and where I'd be staying.

Am I the only person on earth who travels and doesn't make plans about where I'm staying, how long I'm staying, when I'm going, and where else I'm going? He made it seem that way. I did my best to answer his questions: I explained that I was in the Bahamas for two weeks to go island hopping, and I listed the islands I hoped to get to if the weather cooperated.

"But how long will you stay on each island?" the customs agent asked.

"I don't know," I explained yet again. "I've already been held up two days due to the weather; my flying schedule will be dictated by what the sky is looking like each day. So I can't really say how long I'll stay anywhere."

"So it's just you?" he asked.

"Yes, it's just me."

He looked confused. "Then who's the pilot?"

I said, "I told you, I'm the pilot."

He looked more confused. "Are you meeting your husband or boyfriend here?"

Oh boy. "I don't have a husband or boyfriend, and I'm not meeting anyone."

Pause. "So it's just you?"

We went around this circle thrice. I was starting to get the impression that he was sizing me up as a drug runner. Why else would anyone travel *alone* to paradise? My suspicions were confirmed when he began to ask me at length about the contents of my airplane and what I planned to do on the island. He wasn't crazy about me not knowing where I was going to stay, but since I couldn't give him a definite answer, he finally said, exasperated, "Just write down Seacrest."

Finally done with me, the agent stamped the forms with such ferocity that it looked like he was squashing an army of bugs. And this guy had a lot to stamp: my passport, the transire he'd had me fill out (I still didn't know what it was or what I was supposed to do with it), and my cruising permit (which I needed in order to island hop).

I admired the Bahamas stamp in my passport as I walked back to Orion to unload my (non-drug) cargo. The warm air felt wonderful on my skin after this harsh winter. The sky was now clear, and there was a gentle breeze that made Orion's wings rock slightly from side to side. Before I could open the plane door, I got attacked by the no-see-ums—tiny biting bugs common in areas with a lot of water—that I read so much about in Jimmy Buffett's books. I dove for my can of OFF and hosed myself down with it, but in the interim, I got about six mosquito bites and god knows how many no-see-um bites. Welcome to paradise, indeed!

When I exited the airport with my things, I encountered three Biminians sitting outside. One of them, a guy who looked about thirty, immediately struck up a friendly conversation with me, and offered a lot of advice about where to go and what to see.

"Which airline did you come in on?" a woman next to him asked, looking confused. "There are no flights scheduled for this time."

"My own plane," I said.

She gave me one of those *Really? Damn, girl!* looks I often get when I give people that answer. "What do you do for a living?"

"I'm an editor," I said, keeping it simple. Very few people understand what I do when I throw in the financial compliance aspect of my job, so sometimes I skip that part.

"Are you here to write about the Bahamas?" she asked—another response I get all the time. Why do so many think "editor" is the same thing as "writer"? But whatever, I'd go along with this to make things easy. "Yep," I said. "That's why I'm here!" Nothing wrong with people thinking I'm a travel writer—it puts them on their best behavior!

The guy who had first started talking to me got me a cab. He held the door open for me as I slid into the backseat. "Show her the Fountain of Youth," he said to the driver.

I gave him a puzzled look. "Isn't the Fountain of Youth supposed to be in St. Augustine in Florida?"

"You tell me," he said. "I'm ninety years old—do I look it?"

I laughed, thanked him for his help, and said goodbye. When he shut the door, the driver asked me where I was going.

"Seacrest?" I said. Might as well go to the place I'd written down on the customs form; I wasn't sure where else to go.

The driver nodded and pulled away from the curb, and all my muscles tightened as she settled on the wrong side of the one-lane road. I knew to expect that—it's a former British colony, after all—but it still made me tense up. She also blew right past the Fountain of Youth without saying a word; I saw it out of the corner of my eye as we flew past it, though, and I don't think I missed much. From the glimpse I caught, it just looked like a decrepit fountain sitting oddly out of place on the side of the road, surrounded by thick trees.

The driver picked up a friend on the way, and they spoke to one another in English that I couldn't understand. I didn't mind; I enjoyed listening to the rise and fall of the unfamiliar speech from my perch in the backseat. They Americanized it when they addressed me so I could understand what they were saying.

I had to take a water taxi to get to North Bimini, where my hotel was, but even with that, my entire fare so far had only been $5. When we arrived at the dock, I was surrounded immediately by dozens of guys pushing each other to get close to me and yelling "Taxi!"

One approached me calmly in the midst of the shouting. "Hello, I'm Milton," he said. "Do you need a taxi?"

I nodded and went with him—only to find that Seacrest, my chosen hotel, was just across the street from the dock. Milton drove me the twenty or so feet across the street, and in the ten seconds it took us to cross the street and put the car in park, he managed to compliment me multiple times: "A pretty girl like you ... you have such strong legs ..." He also charged me $7 for the "trip."

I was annoyed, but it didn't seem worth it to argue. You win some, you lose some.

I had already sweated out about twice my weight, and there

was no air conditioning in the check-in room (not what I would call a lobby) to this hotel. But luckily there *was* a vacancy. In fact, I was the only one staying there.

"When is the cold weather coming, eh?" the proprietress asked Milton.

"I'm here to escape the cold weather!" I said. "I hope it's not coming at all!" Hot as I was, this beat the freezing temperatures I'd just left behind.

Milton helped me take my luggage up the stairs to my room. "If you need *anything*," he said, and handed me his card.

"Thanks," I said—then ushered him out and closed the door behind him. The lock on the door was a dinky little thing—the kind that you twist a quarter turn in the center of a round doorknob. The door technically also had one of those short chain-lock thingies, too, but it was rusted through—totally unusable. *Good thing crime is nearly non-existent in the islands!* I thought. At least, that was what everyone had told me. I hoped it was true.

AN HOUR AFTER ARRIVING AT MY HOTEL, I WAS WALKING up the only main street, hoping to see what there was to see. There were lots of people just sitting around; I had read that the unemployment rate in the Bahamas was 48 percent, so that didn't come as too much of a surprise.

Everyone I passed was friendly and said hi to me, but I couldn't help but feel that their friendliness was in part because I stuck out like a sore thumb. I took a side street to the other side of the island (it's only about one block wide) to see what was there, and found myself at the edge of a nice beach—free of litter and deserted, just the kind I liked. I walked down to the water and watched the start of the sunset, but as the sun dropped lower on the horizon, I looked back up at the street and noticed two men who seemed to be following me. I decided I should get back to my hotel before dark. I realize that, as a woman traveling alone, I have to be extra careful. I try not to let it worry me to the point that I never go out, but I am always on my guard. It sure doesn't hurt to be, and it's gotten me out of a few scary situations. In this case, I kept looking at them to let them know I saw them and that they couldn't sneak up on me.

I walked along the beach to get back to my hotel, collecting two really cool conch shells on the way. The men, thankfully, walked on when I entered the hotel.

When I found that the restaurant my hotel's proprietress had suggested I go to was closed (you'd think she would have known that), I went wandering up and down the dark street until I found a general store, a sparse room dimly lit by one bare bulb, and asked the old lady working the counter where I could get dinner.

"The only place open is Sara's, on the other side of the island," she said. She stuck her head out the door. "Hey!" she yelled to a friend who was passing by in their car. "Give this lady a ride to Sara's!"

This was my first introduction to the apparently common practice of hitching a ride on the islands. The old lady saw the worried look on my face and said, "He's okay. He works for the electric company."

Uh-huh. I wasn't sure what one had to do with the other, but she didn't look like the type of person to put me in a dangerous situation. And this was an adventure, right? At least, that's what I told myself as I climbed into his car. I also sized him up and figured I could take him if it came to that—he was pretty small.

We passed through what looked like some pretty rough neighborhoods on the way to the restaurant: the buildings all looked bombed out, there were abandoned cars left seemingly where they stopped running, and garbage was piled everywhere. When we arrived, I offered to buy him dinner to thank him, but he politely refused and went on his way.

Sara's was empty except for the two people running things: an older lady, the cook, and a girl in her late teens, possibly her granddaughter, who was helping her. When I walked in they just stared at me and didn't say a word.

"Uh, hi," I said. "I'm hungry?" I wasn't really sure what to say. What did they think I was there for?

The girl stayed where she was seated and pointed to the stack of menus. After a quick perusal, I figured what the hell and ordered fried conch; might as well have a true Bahamian meal my first night in the Bahamas, right?

After I ordered, the older lady suddenly got a curious look on her face. "Are you the girl who flew in on her own plane?" she asked.

Wow. It was a little unnerving that in the span of maybe three hours, word had already gotten to the opposite side of the island. Apparently the coconut telegraph works very quickly in Bimini. I nodded in response, and tried not to show how disconcerted I was that she knew that.

The restaurant reeked of grease, and the fried conch tasted like the place smelled—no salt or other seasonings, just oil. I poured on salt and pepper, the only things available, and squeezed the lime slice that came on the side of the plate all over the strips, but it was still terrible. While I was eating, I eavesdropped on the conversation the two women were having.

"I went to Ft. Lauderdale two weeks ago, you know?" she said. "And at the airport there, there's a Domino's Pizza, Taco

Bell, Panda Express, Church's—every American fast food place you can think of!"

I waited for her to say how lousy it was and ask why can't they have better food there. Wrong.

"When I saw all those great places, I didn't want to leave!" she enthused.

I waited for the older woman to say something about how terrible all that food is—but no. She nodded in agreement.

Seriously? I couldn't believe that they would like fast food that much. Though if all the meals here on Bimini were like the one I was having, I reasoned, fast food would start looking pretty good pretty fast to me, too.

I was just about to leave when who would walk in but my cab driver, Milton. He motioned for me to sit. "Join me," he said.

I had nothing else to do, so I sat with him while he ate—something I regretted as he got further into his meal. He had ordered the snapper, and he ate *the whole thing.* Like, including the head and eyes. He saw me watching him crunch through the bone and smiled. "The head is the best part, you know," he said.

The greasy conch I ate was starting to have an unpleasant conversation with my stomach. I didn't want to be rude, but as soon as he'd finished eating, I stood to leave.

"I'm going to walk back to my hotel, Milton. See you around."

He rose hastily. "No, no," he said. "It's not safe to walk. I will give you a ride!"

Right, I thought. *For a price.*

Milton accepted the money I paid him when we arrived back at the Seacrest, but he wasn't done with me yet.

"Can I keep you company for the evening?" he asked.

"No, I don't think so," I responded firmly.

"But I'll just have to go back to my lonely house on the beach," he lamented. "Please, let me keep you company."

Not interested. I made it as clear as I possibly could that there was no way Milton was coming inside with me—and no way I was going home with him—and finally, after more back and forth than I would have liked, he gave up and let me go.

I dropped onto my bed like a brick when I got back to my room; I was exhausted. But knowing that the whole island knew I was there, and that at least one of them was horny, freaked me out a bit. I remembered the two guys who had followed me earlier, when I was walking on the beach, and I shuddered. I couldn't shake the thought that anyone who wanted to could get my door open by doing little more than breathing on it. I had heard Milton refer to me as "the rich girl" while we were in the restaurant—people always assumed I was rich when they found out I had my own plane—and that made me really uncomfortable. That's not how I wanted to be known around here. I'd known it would be impossible for me to blend in when flying my plane to a relatively poor country, but I didn't like the way I was standing out.

I don't mind being a woman traveling alone—in fact, I actually prefer it in most places, because it offers complete freedom to do what I want to do, when I want to do it, without having to worry about what the other person wants to do. But this place was reminding me too much of the occasional down-falls of being a woman traveling alone. I found myself wishing that Nick hadn't had to bail on the trip. It would have been nice to have a friendly face there. *But he's not here*, I reminded myself, *and you'll be fine. Just go to sleep.*

I tried to listen to myself, but I ended up tossing and turning all night, too wound up to sleep. I hoped that the weather would be good enough for me to leave the next morn-ing. I even figured I'd skip/postpone my run if need be—something that is usually non-negotiable for me—so that I could get out before any potential afternoon storms built up. I had heard such nice things about Bimini, but I was just too uncomfortable to stay. And since the whole "plan"—if you could even call my loose idea of where I wanted to go a plan— for this trip was to stay if I liked a place and go if I didn't, it was time to go. I wanted to be someplace where I could relax, not be on edge and on public display.

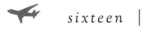 *sixteen* | THE BEST-
LAID PLANS

"*You've got to be very careful if you don't know where you are going,
because you might not get there.*"

—YOGI BERRA

I HESITANTLY TIPTOED TO THE WINDOW TO SEE
what the weather looked like when the sun came up
the next morning, and I was relieved to see that it was
pretty clear—only a few cumulonimbi building up in a direction
I was pretty sure I wasn't going. After taking a taxi from the
airport, a water taxi after that, and then another taxi across the
street, though, I wasn't exactly sure in which direction I was
looking. I decided to be optimistic.

Andros was the closest island to Bimini, about 80 miles
southeast, and it was my next destination. I was curious to see
how it compared to Bimini—from what I was reading in my pilot's
guide, it seemed like it would be much different. *Fingers crossed.*

Andros is the largest yet most sparsely populated Bahamian island. It's 2,300 square miles, a huge contrast to the other
islands in the Bahamas, most of which are only a few miles
long. Andros is also home to the world's third-largest barrier
reef, called the "Tongue of the Ocean." Like Bimini, Andros

was originally inhabited by the Lucayan Indians, also known as "the invisible people" because of the mud they covered themselves with. I don't know who they were hiding from before the Europeans showed up, but apparently the mud proved fairly useful—after visiting the island, the Europeans reported seeing evidence of inhabitants but never seeing the inhabitants themselves. The island was then "discovered" in 1550, when the Spanish came in search of slave labor; they took the liberty of renaming it "La Isla del Espíritu Santo" (The Island of the Holy Spirit) while they were at it.

Andros has three airports: north, central, and south. My pilot's guide said that San Andros, the north airport, had fuel—there didn't appear to be anything else there, however, so I figured I'd stop there, fuel up, and fly on to Andros Town, the central airport, to visit a batik factory that offered tours and spend the night before moving on.

Flying over Andros, I could see evidence of its sparse population: it was all dense greenery, save for just a few small roads crisscrossing the island. No villages in sight, no houses—just the airport and roads that looked to me like they led to nowhere.

They say you should always call ahead to places that supposedly have fuel in the Bahamas. In this case, I stupidly chose to ignore that suggestion. I assumed that since the pilots' guide I bought was updated every year, the information must be accurate. Right?

There wasn't a person in sight when I landed at North Andros Airport. It was so desolate that if the islands had tumbleweed, I'm convinced some would have blown past, accompanied by that three-note, eerie trill that always plays when the bad guys show up in Westerns. I studied the small buildings at the edge of the tarmac. Did one look more like a customs office than the others? Was there even anyone here? I couldn't tell.

I decided to explore until I found something—or someone. I walked around the first building: no unlocked door. I tried the next building: Bingo! Customs office.

I entered to find the office equally as deserted as the rest of the airport, though I could hear a voice somewhere. I followed the sound to a closed door and knocked on it tentatively. *If I were a customs officer on such a deserted island and heard a plane coming in,* I thought, *I would perhaps get out of my chair and go to see what the plane was there for.* But I ignored my thoughts and put a smile on my face as I poked my head in the door.

The officer put his phone call on hold when he saw me. *Oh, so they get the working phones,* I thought, *and they leave the ones with terrible connections for the pilots trying to call Flight Service so they don't send out a search party!*

"Hi there," I said.

"Hi," he said. "What brings you here?" He said it as if it was ridiculous for me to have landed there.

"To get some fuel?" I said hopefully.

"We haven't had fuel here in about a year," he said matter-of-factly.

Shit. Do I even have enough fuel to get to another island? I wondered, feeling a bit frantic. Bimini didn't have fuel either, so I hadn't fueled up since Florida. I did a quick calculation: I still had about three hours of fuel left but hadn't figured up how long it would take me to get to the next island that had fuel. Picturing the map in my head, I did some estimating and figured I'd make it. *Jesus H. That's a lucky break.*

"So it's just you?" he asked—and thus began the same rigmarole I'd gone through with the first customs agent on Bimini ("You said you're the pilot?!" "Where is your boyfriend?").

Apparently I was the first woman in the history of the universe to ever go to the Bahamas alone, let alone to fly her own plane there. As I answered the agent's questions, I thought, *Note to self: get a tattoo on your forehead that says "Yes, it's just me!" to save time and breath in the future.*

Finally, his curiosity appeased, the customs officer stamped my cruising permit, and I walked back to the plane to figure out where to go next. I really hadn't thought that far ahead, since I thought I'd be in Andros for at least one night, if not longer, so now I was at a bit of a loss as to what to do next. The customs officer had suggested Nassau, which was the next island to the east and the most popular tourist destination in the Bahamas. But I was trying to avoid the super touristy places. What I really wanted was to go to Eleuthera, the next island to the east past Nassau. Luckily it was about 90 miles away, well within what was left of my fuel range. I decided to go there. I'd pass over Nassau along the way, a comforting thought in case I ran into trouble and needed to land. And the customs officer assured me that North Eleuthera Airport had fuel.

I used the airport phone, full of static but not as bad as the one in Bimini, to call for another weather briefing since I hadn't looked at anything past Andros, and got the same "few clouds at 2,500 feet" message that I was to hear every time I called for weather while in the Bahamas (and which, for the record, was untrue every time). I had walked back to Orion and was just finishing up sending my parents a ping from my SPOT GPS to let them know where I was and that I was okay when I looked up to see a guy slowly approaching me. His mouth agape, he looked at my plane, then at me, then back at the plane, then back at me. I wasn't sure what to make of this, so I just stood there waiting as he drew closer.

He stopped a few feet away from me. "Hiiiiiiii!" he said, an expression of excitement—or maybe shock?—on his face. "It's so good to see you!"

Uh-huh. I decided to play along. "Well, hey, man, it's good to see you, too!"

He took another step forward, grabbed my hand, and shook it vigorously. "It's *so good to see you!*" he said again, stressing the words.

"Hey, it's good to see you, too, man!" I responded. I figured if he was going to repeat himself, I might as well do it too—though I did wonder how this would end. *Am I going to get stuck here having the same two-sentence conversation with this guy for the rest of my life?* I wondered.

Luckily, he moved on. "How long have you been here?"

"About ten minutes," I said. "Just long enough to clear customs."

"It's nice to get a visitor," he said. "We don't get many people flying in since the boss quit carrying fuel." He sounded forlorn. I understood. This place felt like a ghost town. "Where are you going next?" he asked.

"Eleuthera," I said. "In fact, I'm about to head there now."

"Right now?" he asked. He looked *absolutely devastated.* "Oh no! Please don't go! I can show you around the island! You can stay at my place! Don't you want to see the island? Please let me show you around! Please just don't go!"

"Thank you for the offer, but I don't think so," I said, a little embarrassed by his intensity.

"Please!" he said. "Just one night!"

If I let this go on any longer, I thought, *he may get down on his knees to beg!* I couldn't let it come to that. "Maybe I'll stop here on my way back to the States," I said, hoping that would appease him.

His face brightened. "Oh, yes!" he said. "Come back before you leave!"

I promised to think about it, and he finally let me leave. But he didn't move a muscle as I climbed into Orion and began to taxi down the runway; he stood rooted in the same place, watching me. As I took off into the wind, I looked back and saw him still standing there and waving sadly. I waved my wings at him as a friendly goodbye.

My new friend was a little overeager, but it was nice to get such a hearty welcome nonetheless. I hoped that people would be this friendly—and harmless—on Eleuthera!

 *seventeen* | A HUNK
OF
BALLAST

"*Go to heaven for the climate, hell for the company.*"
—MARK TWAIN

"SKYHAWK FIVE NINER ZERO SIERRA PAPA, JUST off San Andros, 1,500 climbing 3,500, would like VFR flight following to North Eleuthera please." I was radioing Nassau approach now that I was airborne.

The woman on the other end—who appeared to be half asleep—gave me a squawk code (a unique four-number code I enter into my transponder that makes it easier for them to identify me) and then asked my enroute altitude, which I had already told her.

"Zero sierra papa, 3,500," I answered. Pause.

"Zero sierra papa, verify destination: Governor's Harbour," she said.

"Zero sierra papa, negative," I said. I was getting exasperated now. "Destination: North Eleuthera." *Damn, lady!* I could dig one question, but she had missed half my transmission. *Go get some coffee and then let's try this again*, I thought.

Of course, once I got close to Nassau, the clouds got in my way, so I had to check back in and ask for 5,500.

I got a blasé "pilot's discretion" answer from her, essentially saying, "Whatever you want. Don't bother me."

In the next fifteen minutes I asked for three more altitude changes because clouds kept getting in my way. I'm sure she thought I was bipolar or something, but honestly, you really can't tell where cloud groups are until you're close—not to mention the fact that they form in minutes and are constantly changing! For the third day in a row, I was glad that the VFR rules in the Bahamas were more lax than those in the States: in the air, as long as you were clear of clouds (as in, not currently in a cloud), you were VFR. At this point it was either keep going or turn back, and since the only things within range behind me were one island with no fuel and another with people that scared the shit out of me, I wasn't turning back. There was no one else on the frequency in my sector, nor anyone flying in or out of North Eleuthera, and I could see very well, so I felt okay flying so low with clouds all around.

There was one thing that was a little off, however: every ten minutes or so, I would get a few seconds of an odd and extremely loud sound in my headset that drowned out incoming transmissions. I had to ask the controller, who seemed already peeved that I had actually made her work by entering her airspace, to "say again" a couple of times because of the noise. I hadn't ever heard the sound before. *Maybe I left my cell phone on,* I thought, *or maybe there's something weird in this airspace or on this frequency that's causing it.* My cell phone was buried deep in one of my bags, so I couldn't check on that theory. *Oh well,* I thought, brushing it off. *I'll figure it out later.*

As I neared Eleuthera, it became clear that this particular island couldn't be mistaken for any other island in the chain. It is 110 miles long, but only 2 miles wide at its widest point, which makes most of it look like a sliver carved out of the ocean. Eleuthera's original inhabitants, the Tainos or Arawaks, were taken by the Spanish to work the mines of Hispaniola, where they all died by 1550. Eleuthera was then most likely uninhabited until the first European settlers, the Puritan Pilgrims, arrived from Bermuda around 1649, fleeing religious persecution.

The name "Eleuthera" is a modification of the Greek word for "freedom," since that is what the Europeans were seeking when they fled Bermuda. Infighting among the original settlers soon developed, however, and some fled by boat from the central part of the island for the northern and southern areas. Those going north wrecked on a reef called the Devil's Backbone. Yikes. Thankfully, the airport had a nice, neutral name, North Eleuthera Airport, that didn't make me fear sudden death.

AFTER LANDING IN A LIGHT DRIZZLE, I PULLED ONTO THE ramp and saw a line guy giving me taxi hand signals. I've never been quite sure why they feel it's necessary to give small-plane pilots those signals. If you just stand in front of where you want me to park, I'm pretty sure I can figure out which way to turn the plane to get it there without the hand signals. The line guy did look a bit like Magnum, P.I., however. *Hm,* I thought. *Island fling with a sexy airport dude?* Then I noticed his wedding band. *Damn.*

In the terminal, I asked the FBO receptionist where I should stay, and she suggested a small hotel called Romora Bay on Harbour Island—or "Briland," as the locals call it—another island in the Eleuthera chain just a short water taxi ride away. She said there weren't any hotels around North Eleuthera. I had read that Briland was pretty cool, so I took her advice and made my way there.

Briland, which at one time was the capital of the Bahamas,

is about three and a half miles long by one and a half miles wide
and sits about two miles off mainland Eleuthera. The island's
only town, Dunmore Town, was established by the Loyalist
Governor of Virginia after he fled the Revolutionary War in the
United States. He was awarded the title Lord Dunmore,
Governor of the Bahamas, seemingly for no other reason than
for showing up. I wondered if they were still giving away titles
these days. I wouldn't mind if they wanted to give me one.

AFTER A GLORIOUSLY SAFE-FEELING NIGHT OF SOUND
sleep—thanks to a working lock on the door and no creepy
suitors—I woke up refreshed and ready to explore the island. It
was my first day of not flying after four days of some pretty
intense flying, and while I never thought the day would come
when I wouldn't want to get up in the air, I found myself
relieved to have a break from worrying about the weather,
schlepping luggage, and wondering what I was going to do if
the airport I was going to didn't have fuel.

By the time I came back from my morning run—on the
lovely pink sand beach that was just a few blocks from my hotel
—I already knew that Eleuthera was my favorite island so far. It
was a gloriously sunny, hot day, I had slept well, and my hotel
was adorable: the "rooms" were actually small houses, each one
brightly painted in different colors and outfitted with two
Adirondack chairs on the small porch. Gorgeous tropical flowers
of all colors—such a welcome sight to me from the bleakness of
winter—adorned the grounds, and a talking parrot named Goldie
presided from her large cage and talked to the people passing by
on the stone walkway that led down to a restaurant at the edge
of the water.

Not too far from Romora Bay Hotel was a burger joint that my Bahamas guidebook said was the supposed inspiration of Jimmy Buffett's "Cheeseburger in Paradise." The story went that he had been on a boat for a long time with terrible food, and then he arrived at Harbour Island, where he went to this place and had a cheeseburger good enough to inspire a song.

Truthfully, the burger was one of the worst I've ever had. There was just something ... not ... *right* about it. Something tasted off. The only way it would have been remotely good was if I had been adrift on a stranded boat for about a week and was near starvation. But the family that owned the place was super friendly, and when the daughter found out that I had flown there in my own plane from New Orleans, she was so impressed that she told literally everyone who walked by: "This lady flew her *own plane* here from the *United States!*"

All the attention was making me uncomfortable at first— right up until it brought a cute Italian guy to my table. Alfredo was friends with the owners, and he'd showed up just to say hi, but when the daughter told him about my plane and introduced us, he stayed to chat.

Alfredo had such a thick Italian accent that I had a little trouble understanding him, but he was quite charming and funny, with a sexy, deep voice like the character Emile de Becque in *South Pacific*. *Now this is* exactly *why I like to be a woman traveling solo!* I thought as the minutes ticked by and Alfredo continued to sit with me, entertaining me with his stories. We were talking about flying, of course, so he told me about his first trip in an airplane—from Italy, when he was eighteen—and then he told me about his worst trip in an airplane.

"The turbulence was terrible," he said. "We were bouncing up and down. And then we hit a ... what you call it? Air socket?"

I stifled a laugh. "Yeah, something like that."

"But I have never been in a small plane before," he said. "Only the big jets."

"Would you like me to take you up for a ride tomorrow?" I offered.

His face lit up. "That would be wonderful!"

I was thoroughly enjoying his company, so I was glad when Alfredo offered to walk me to a shop that I'd read about in my pilots' guide. But as soon as we exited the restaurant, he spotted a friend driving slowly past on a golf cart, and he flagged him down and asked if he could give us a ride.

A ride? I thought, incredulous. The shop wasn't that far. But he was already on the cart, so I hopped up beside him. As we putted slowly along, I noticed that *everyone* seemed to be on a golf cart, and no one was on foot. It was like the locals had an aversion to walking.

"You see that?" Alfredo asked, interrupting my thoughts. I looked where he was pointing—across Exuma Sound, the body of water separating Harbour Island from mainland Eleuthera.

"What am I looking for?" I asked.

"I'm building a restaurant there," he said.

Hmm ... a sexy and charming Italian restaurateur? This could definitely get interesting! Alfredo was a little bit old for me—my guess was that he was about fifty—but hey, I was on vacation.

After I was done shopping, Alfredo took his leave.

"I need to take care of a few things at home," he said, "but I would like to see you later. Will you have a drink with me tonight?"

"I would love to," I said.

He said he could catch the last water ferry to meet me at my hotel later that evening, and he gave me his number and told me to call him in a few hours to confirm. We shook hands in front of a decrepit fruit and vegetable stand on the waterfront, and then we hugged. Both of us held on longer than necessary. *Here we go*, I thought.

ONCE I GOT BACK TO MY HOTEL, I TRIED TO CALL Alfredo, but the call wouldn't go through from my cell. I had told him earlier that I might have trouble reaching him—all my previous calls had proven unsuccessful so far ever since I left Florida, so I didn't really expect it to work. But now I wasn't sure what to do. There was no way to reach him.

I hoped Alfredo would realize I couldn't get in touch with him and would come over anyway. I thought he had said that the water taxi from Eleuthera to Harbour Island only ran during daylight hours, so I figured if he wasn't there by 6 p.m., he wasn't coming. I sat on the Adirondack on my porch to wait for him and watch the sunset, I started to get a little bummed out even though I wasn't totally sure I wanted him to come. I was always on the lookout for a hot guy, but I also wanted this to be an enjoyable vacation, free from worrying if some guy liked me or not or if he'd do what he said he'd do. On the one hand, I felt like I wouldn't mind an island fling; but on the other hand, I didn't want the hassle. This trip was supposed to be about relaxing, forgetting about work, and exploring new places. *Not some guy.*

At 6 p.m., no Alfredo in sight, I went back inside my room to freshen up. *I'll go to dinner and call it an early night*, I decided, feeling lower and lower by the minute. We had agreed before parting ways that afternoon that if I didn't see him that night, he'd pick me up at the dock at Eleuthera at eleven the next morning so I could take him flying, but now I was even beginning to wonder about that. *Will he even show up?* I wondered.

A little depressed now, I walked down to the hotel restaurant at the bottom of the hill. *Don't let this mess up your evening,* I chastised myself. *He didn't show; so what?* I hadn't planned to do any sort of dating on this vacation anyway. Why let some guy get in my head? But he kinda had.

My stomach was hurting, like something wasn't agreeing with me, but I was hungry, and hunger wins out every time—so I ordered some jerk chicken wings, one of my favorite Caribbean dishes. I was the only person in the whole restaurant who was sitting alone. Normally that wouldn't bother me, but tonight it did. I faced away from the other occupied tables (all two of them) and just looked out at the water, though I couldn't see much. *Why is it so damned dark at night here?* My mood was bordering on petulant now.

I had just finished the chicken and was waiting for the waiter to come by so I could ask for the check when I saw a shadow coming up behind me. *Phew, finally!* I thought. The waiter had been MIA for what felt like ages by this point. I turned to ask for the check—and then flinched when I realized it was Alfredo. *Shit,* I thought, and looked down at my already-eaten plate of food. *I should have waited for him.*

"Didn't you get the messages I left for you at the front desk?" he asked, reading my surprise.

"Messages?"

"Yes, I left two," he said.

"I guess they forgot to tell me," I said. *Thanks a lot, guys.*

Alfredo sat down with me and ordered a Kalik, a Bahamian beer. Now I was getting a little nervous because he was really here, smelled dangerously and intoxicatingly good, and was making me laugh a lot. I warned myself not to be lured in by his smell. I tried to focus on the fact that he also smelled of smoke, which served as kind of an antidote to the sexy cologne. It surprised me to realize just how many of my personal rules I was breaking so far: 1) too old; 2) smoker; 3) total stranger in a strange place who could kill me and I'd never be heard from again.

Our conversation was more serious than it had been at lunch. I asked him more about his restaurant and got an earful. He had been working on it for three years. A business partner/ very recent ex-girlfriend owned the land, but he had signed a ninety-nine-year lease and built a house that stood there now.

"Why did you break up?" I asked, curious.

"We were together for two years," he said, "and I loved her."

"And then?" I prompted.

"Then she stole money from me—thousands of dollars, right out of my wallet," he said. "All my friends had warned me that she was a pathological liar"—everyone on these islands knows everything about everyone else—"and didn't really care about me. It took me a long time to see the truth."

"What made you finally end things?" I asked.

"I caught her stealing from me again two weeks ago, and that was it," he said.

We sat and talked for a while longer, and Alfredo explained that he was actually leaving on Wednesday to go back to Italy for an indefinite visit. He was more than ready to return home. He'd had enough of island life, needed to get away from his ex, and needed to think about what to do with the restaurant. Apparently he couldn't get power wired to his property without paying bribes, and he said he would not participate in anything that was not strictly legit.

I had to appreciate his morals, but I couldn't help but weigh in. "That's just how things work on the islands," I said. "You have to play the game." I had read a number of books about the islands, including the very realistic novel *Don't Stop the Carnival* —a story about a guy who bought a hotel on an island and went crazy because of how backward he felt everything was there and how nothing ever seemed to get accomplished. The novel was based on the author's real-life experiences as a hotel owner on a Caribbean island, so I trusted that it was realistic. I felt for Alfredo, I really did, but one determined Italian was not going change how business in the Bahamas was done.

Alfredo nodded sadly. "Yes. It's a ... what you call it? A catch-fifty-four."

I snorted and then choked on the water I was drinking at that one. But I didn't correct him.

The mosquitoes were eating us alive, so we decided to go back to my room. When we got inside, I told him I needed a shower.

"I will go to get a coffee from the hotel café so you can have some time alone," he said immediately, and was out the door.

I thought his actions were polite and gentlemanly. *Maybe he just needs a smoke*, my cynical side chimed in. But I decided to give him the benefit of the doubt.

I was in my towel drying off, trying to find some cutesy clothes to wear—not easy, since this was a vacation on which I hadn't planned to need any cutesy clothes—when Alfredo returned. *I should have listened to Patti*, I thought. She was an old friend and flight instructor and she'd told me she had no doubt I would pick up—I love how she worded this—a "hunk of ballast." At the time I thought, *Yeah, right!* But here I was, in my towel, a handsome Italian man standing before me in my hotel room.

I gave Alfredo a nonchalant "Hi." What else to do at this point? It wasn't exactly normal for a first date to see me in a towel, but it was happening, so I figured I might as well go with it. We talked a little more sitting next to each other on the bed, and we had a few moments where all we did was look at each other and smile. Of course, sitting so close, I could smell him again. That smell. God, that smell. *I ... can ... resist*, I told myself. But then he kissed me. *So much for resisting!*

We had that awkward first-time sex that is really more of a kind of hurdle to overcome than anything else. There was nothing out of the ordinary with my same-day-as-we-met Italian lover. I had half expected some really mind-blowing sex. But even amidst the awkwardness, I definitely saw potential.

Afterward, we lay in bed and just looked at each other a lot. Every so often he would squint kind of sexily, and I had a feeling he was trying to read my mind. It was nice. But then he said to me out of nowhere, "Don't fall in love."

Wha?! That was an odd thing to say! When did *love* enter the picture? This was sex. *Just sex.* I didn't want to share that I had broken up with my past two boyfriends because they fell in love with me alarmingly fast. I also didn't want to say that there wasn't a snowball's chance in hell of me falling in love with him. But because I was so shocked by his statement, all I said was, "Wellll, alrighty then!"

Alfredo fell asleep before I did, and his snoring was loud enough to wake the dead in a universe light years away. Is there such a thing as a guy who doesn't snore? If so, I haven't found him yet, but Alfredo ranked up there with the worst of them. I was miserable. Even with earplugs in, I could hear him; the bed and pillow were vibrating.

I laughed to myself again about his comment. I couldn't *possibly* fall in love with this guy—and what a stupid thing that he even thought there was a *remote* possibility! Ha! He smoked, snored, drank too much, was too old, lived too far away, and was on the rebound. Sounded like a pretty perfect formula for *not* falling in love to me!

IN THE MORNING, I OPENED MY EYES TO SEE ALFREDO already out of bed and putting his shorts on.

"Good morning," he said when he saw me watching him. "I must go home, but I will see you at the Eleuthera dock at eleven, yes?"

"Sure," I said, "see you there."

He left without giving me even a peck on the cheek. *Typical end to a one-night stand*, I thought.

I had my running clothes on and had just eaten my breakfast Pop Tarts when I heard a gurgle come from my stomach. *Something is very wrong*, I realized. There was no way I was going running; there was no way I was going *anywhere*. I thought about the previous day's meals, and could only assume that the "cheeseburger in paradise" was the culprit. I couldn't believe it. I had *major* food poisoning. On my vacation. In paradise. With a flying date in four hours. *Well, at least it held out long enough for me to have sex.*

Between trips to the bathroom, I had the hotel receptionist patch a call through to Alfredo to tell him that there was no way I could take him flying. He was hard enough to understand in person but even more so over the phone.

"Why can't you go?" he asked more than once. "What is wrong?" I think he thought I was lying to get out of seeing him again. I kept telling him that I felt terrible and was super sick and dizzy, and finally he said okay.

"Call me later, okay?" he said.

"Okay," I agreed. I still wasn't sure if he understood me, but I was grateful to get off the phone. The bathroom was calling my name.

I spent most of the day thinking that I was really screwed. Here I was in the middle of nowhere (the island didn't even show a name on the map when I pinged my dad with the SPOT and he clicked the link to see where I was), with no one to take care of me, no medication, no crackers or chicken soup or any of the usual comfort foods you need when you're sick, and no way to leave until I felt 100 percent since *I* was my only means of transportation. And there were no doctors on the island. That realization scared me. I also heard from the hotel staff that just a couple of weeks earlier a woman had gotten so sick that she'd had to be Medivac'd off the island to get proper medical care. I wondered how many people had an emergency and couldn't wait for the Medivac. That scared me even more. I just hoped my sickness would pass and that I wouldn't get to that point.

After spending the entire day in bed, I was feeling marginally better, and I decided that there was no way I was going to let this sickness ruin my vacation. I called Alfredo to tell him I thought I'd be okay for the next morning. I mean, this could be the kind of summer fling ("winter fling" just doesn't have the same ring to it) that I'd tell my grandkids about, with a faraway, longing look in my eyes, when I was too old to have summer flings—right? I decided I was going to get well overnight, come hell or high water. Alfredo and I agreed to stick with our original plan, just one day later, and meet at the Eleuthera dock at eleven the next morning, by which time I was determined to be feeling just fine, dammit.

I TOOK MY TIME GETTING READY THE FOLLOWING morning and hesitantly ate a Pop Tart to start to get my energy back while I packed my bags. Life (and this vacation) was too short to be sick, so I'd better get back to normal as fast as I could. Plus, I had a date! What better excuse to coax my body back to normal? Alfredo had said that I could stay at his place that night, so I assumed that's where I'd be. I knew he didn't have any electricity, but he said the breeze at night kept it cool enough to sleep.

By the time I left my hotel, it had started to drizzle and the clouds were getting darker. It was pouring when I got on the water taxi, and as we pulled up to Three Islands Dock in Eleuthera, it started to come down even harder. I gathered my luggage, doing my best to cover the bag with my computer in it, and ran to the bar where Alfredo said he'd be waiting. I—and my stuff—was soaked.

I didn't see Alfredo in the tiny shack, but, knowing that everyone knew him, I turned to the closest guy to me.

"Do you know where Alfredo is?"

He wordlessly pointed to the even tinier room within the bar.

I found Alfredo in there smoking like crazy, of course, and drinking a beer at eleven thirty in the morning. *Right. I should have known.*

The whole scene was surreal and seemed like it came from a movie. The rain poured down outside—lots of it coming through the palm frond roof of the bar—and the locals were gathered around the TV absolutely riveted by a really lousy B-movie. A lone poster of Derek Jeter hung on the wall. I was soaking wet, and there was Alfredo, having a smoke and a beer.

"I don't think we're going to go flying anytime soon," I said, sitting down.

"What would you like to do?" he asked, tapping his cigarette on the ashtray in front of him.

"I don't know," I said. "You're the one who lives here!"

Apparently there weren't many options. We could either sit there at the bar or sit someplace else. Other than taking in the natural beauty of these islands, there was little, if anything, else to do, especially since we didn't have any wheels. So we sat for a while. My stomach was still gurgling a lot and seemed tentative at best, so I didn't want to test its resilience yet by drinking. At least the breeze from the storm was keeping Alfredo's smoke away from me while we sat and watched the rain inside and outside.

"It doesn't look like this rain is going to clear up any time soon," I finally said, growing bored with our surroundings. "Flying will have to wait for another day. Should we go back to your place?"

He called the one taxi on the island. It was only a few blocks to get to his house; it would have been walkable in better weather. He opened the front door, and I walked into a house that was also a very empty future restaurant. Downstairs, there was a small bar and room for about six small tables with chairs. All the chairs were upside down on the tables except for the two tables closest to the kitchen. I could tell immediately that those were the ones he used because they had a pile of cigarette butts and ashes under them. The place was pretty clean except for the mixture of sand and cigarette ashes covering the floor of the entire downstairs, which swirled up and temporarily clouded the air in the room every time a door opened. The kitchen only had a few pots and pans, plates, and glasses. There was also a smallish refrigerator. The grill was nice, but I just couldn't foresee this tiny kitchen ever serving as a restaurant kitchen, even for a restaurant this small.

On the beach side of the kitchen was a door that led out to a nice-sized deck and steps to the beach. About six feet from the bottom of the steps, the water lapped at the sand. It really was quite nice and would be a beautiful setting for a restaurant —if Alfredo ever got to open it.

Upstairs were two small bedrooms, each with a full bathroom and a balcony on both sides. One room was completely empty; the other only had a mattress on the floor and a small cabinet with a PVC pipe in it to hang his clothes on. He had very few personal items there: maybe a dozen shirts, a nice suit, a few pairs of fancy Italian shoes, some cologne (damn that seductive stuff!), and a few toiletries. I'm a light packer, yet I had more stuff in my luggage than he had in his entire house. *How has he lived like this for three years?!* I wondered.

"All the furniture belongs to my ex-girlfriend," Alfredo said as he saw me inspecting the room. "I have asked her many times to come to get her things before I leave, so I can board up the house when I go, but she will not answer my phone calls. I hope she will come soon."

We went back downstairs, and since he knew I thought conch shells were cool, he told me about a live conch that he had caught recently in the water right in front of his house and cooked.

"As I was eating it, I bit down on something hard. I took it out of my mouth and still didn't know what it was. It was small and pink, kind of egg-shaped. The next day, I asked a local guy who was working on my house about it, and you know what he told me?"

"What?"

"It was a conch pearl!" Alfredo said.

"I had no idea conch made pearls," I said. "How interesting!"

"I didn't know either," he said. He reached into his pocket and, turning my palm over, he dropped the pearl into my hand. "You have it," he said—quite unceremoniously, like it was no big deal.

I thought it was a really nice gesture—and because of that, I suddenly grew a bit puzzled as to what was going on with us.

There was the whole "don't fall in love" thing, but now he was giving me a really rare and totally unexpected gift. *Hmm. Odd.*

All day, we sat on the steps to the beach and watched the tide come in while we talked. That afternoon, we took a cab to a grocery store so we could get what we needed to make dinner. I was just hoping that my still-churning stomach could handle dinner. It was probably best that we hadn't been able to fly, since my stomach was still in pretty bad shape. We had skipped lunch altogether, so I wasn't sure how my stomach would react to a full meal. But I didn't want to ask Alfredo to change his dinner plan just because I was still recovering. I mean, how often does an Italian restaurateur offer to cook for you? I decided to deal, come what may.

When we got back to his house, Alfredo cranked up the generator and got to work on our meal. He was making pasta carbonara, and he whipped up the egg mixture in a bowl with some spices and put that aside for later, then started tending to the next step.

I hated just standing there not doing a thing to help. "Should I put on some music?" I suggested. *Music is help, right?* "I have Vivaldi!" I figured he would go well with our Italian meal and my Italian date.

"Yes, music sounds good," Alfredo said, so I got out my computer and plugged it in close to where we would sit to eat. I was looking for Vivaldi when I saw the front door open out of the corner of my eye. I didn't think anything of it—I figured someone had just come by for a friendly visit. But in walked a large Bahamian woman and two men in what looked like customs officers' uniforms. I thought for a second that I was in trouble. *I haven't flown in days—what could I have possibly done?* I wondered. But then I made out the word "Police" on their badges. Not customs, then. I wondered what they were doing there.

If this had happened back in the States, I would have been freaking out, but it seemed like just another part of this odd island life, so I barely batted an eyelash. After what felt like the gold medal record in uncomfortable silences, one of the officers finally spoke:

"Is Alfredo home?"

I turned back to look at him in the kitchen and realized he was still busy cooking and hadn't heard them come in.

"Alfredo?" I called out to him.

He looked at me, waiting for what I was going to say, and I pointed at the guys he couldn't see from where he was standing and said, "Company."

The woman immediately barged past me and started taking stuff. *Ah, so this is the ex,* I thought, finally putting two and two together. *But what's with the cops?*

Most of the stuff was hers, but she also started to take some that wasn't. She wanted the bowl Alfredo had just made the sauce in, so she took it and dumped the sauce down the sink.

"Wait! That's mine!" he protested. She shrugged and threw the now-empty bowl back into the sink with a clang. Meanwhile, I kept an eye on my luggage by the door, nervous that she might try to take my stuff, too. She was certainly on a roll.

Crazy Ex stormed upstairs, and Alfredo followed her to make sure she didn't take his stuff. I hung out next to my luggage by the door, trying to look nonchalant.

One of the cops turned to me after they'd been upstairs for a couple of minutes and asked, "Is everything okay?"

Seriously? I laughed nervously and said, "I sure as hell don't know! You tell me!"

Ultimately, all Crazy Ex took that night after throwing a few things around for dramatic effect (it worked!) was a small

TV, a coffee maker, and the pot Alfredo was about to use to cook the pasta.

He asked her why she brought the police officers.

"I didn't want any trouble," she responded.

"*What* trouble?" he asked. "I've been *begging* you to come get your stuff for weeks!"

She moved to leave.

"Why aren't you taking all of your stuff?" he asked, confused.

"I'll be back for it," she huffed.

"But when?" he asked. He clearly wanted to be done with this drama.

"It's my place," she said, "and I can come whenever I please."

Alfredo kept his cool—something I would have lost completely by that point. "It most certainly is *not* your place," he said, "and you'd better let me know before you come here again."

She didn't respond—she just spun around and stormed out the door, the police quietly and subserviently in tow.

I looked at Alfredo with raised eyebrows when they were gone. "Wow."

"I am sorry," he said. "I suspected that she might show up tonight, but I hoped she wouldn't. She called earlier to say she was coming, and I asked if she could come some other time since I have company, but she just hung up."

A little warning would have been nice, I thought. But what I said was, "Should I be worried that she'll come back here to start trouble with me?"

"No, no, she would not do that," he assured me.

"How can you know that?" I asked. "You seemed pretty surprised at her behavior just now—the throwing things around and bringing the police. What if she surprises you again?"

"It will be okay," Alfredo assured me. "She will not come back tonight."

I was still a little nervous. *Just remember how little crime there is in the islands,* I told myself. I just hoped I wouldn't be that rare Bahamian crime statistic!

Now we had nothing to cook in. We tried to think of something we could use to boil water, but there was nothing in the house that would work. So Alfredo, after a long sigh, called another cab to go back to the grocery store. He returned with a skillet and a pot and started from the beginning, smoking like a chimney as he worked. He was noticeably perturbed over the business with the Crazy Ex.

It would have been a wonderful dinner under any circumstances, but it was much more so considering what little Alfredo had to work with and the fact that he did it all on generator power only. He even made it a little spicy just for me since I told him I like spicy food. I decided to skip the wine because of my still-churning stomach, but the food, thankfully, I did just fine with.

Once we finished eating, I changed the music on my computer from classical music to random stuff and started to groove to it while we were sitting and talking.

"Why don't you get up to dance?" he asked.

"*Hell* no!" I said. "I would have to be drunk to even think about dancing—and then I would regret it later, as soon as I was sober."

I thought the matter was settled there—but wouldn't you know it, Alfredo put his odd magical powers to work, and within minutes I was doing something I thought I'd never do: I was dancing to every song that came on, completely sober. Sometimes he was dancing right in front of me; sometimes we were doing our own thing across the room while laughing at each other's stupid moves. Then, when I put on "Besame Mucho," he attempted to get me to dance with him, bless his heart. I kept laughing when he would go one way and I would go the other way. I'm a terrible follower and can never pick up on those subtle cues men give when they lead. But I had to admit that it was a bit intoxicating when it worked. I could see our reflection in the windows, and I smiled at how surprised I was about everything. It had been an interesting night by many counts. This would *indeed* be the kind of fling I would day-dream about longingly when I was too old to have them!

We went to bed after a while, and again we talked for hours, mostly me asking him about his business situation and what led to his breakup. Finally, at 2:30 a.m., we were done talking, and he started to caress me and kiss me—but then he stopped.

"Don't stop," I said. "I won't be able to sleep!"

But he had already passed out.

I shook him awake. "Why did you stop?" I asked, trying to keep the annoyance I was feeling out of my voice.

"It didn't seem like you were that into it," he said, his voice muffled by his pillow.

Hell, we were just getting started! I was definitely into it! I was pissed. But Alfredo was already snoring again. How easily, after our fun day together, I had forgotten about the snoring. *This is it*, I thought. *I don't need this. What the hell am I doing here, anyway?*

After about an hour of lying there and fuming, I jammed earplugs into my ears as far as they would go and—only because I was completely exhausted—I finally fell asleep. And was promptly awakened by what sounded like a goddamn hurricane outside. Normally I find the sound of a rainstorm very sooth-ing, and I tried to go back to sleep, but I started to worry about my airplane. It was *really* blowing out there. And I knew most airports in the Bahamas didn't have tiedowns to secure planes with. *What if Orion flips over in the wind?* I couldn't for the life of me remember if I had seen tiedowns at North Eleuthera Airport when I parked. Naturally, I was too distracted by that cute line guy with the sexy accent. Damn my weakness for men!

I tried to picture my plane in my mind now. Were there ropes tying it down or not? I couldn't remember. I thought there were, but was that just hope? Was I just picturing what I wanted to see as I listened to this storm that I knew could easily blow it over if it didn't have something holding it down? My rising discontent with the entire situation—man and weather—kept me awake.

I sat on the edge of the bed and listened to the wind raging and watched the waves crashing and the trees bending and worried myself into a perfect tizzy. I breathed heavily and sighed again and again in an attempt to wake Alfredo up. *If I have to be so miserable and unable to sleep, he damn well should be, too.* But he just kept snoring away.

I thought for the hundredth time that night how screwed I was if Orion really had flipped over. My plane was my only mode of getting the hell out of here—which, right now, was all I wanted to do. Why did I keep getting myself into these dodgy situations?

AT FIRST LIGHT, STILL AWAKE BUT LYING ON MY SIDE, faced to the wall, I heard Alfredo wake up and go downstairs. The storm had calmed down, but I hadn't. I lay in bed a little while longer, trying to go back to sleep, but it was a lost cause; I gave up and put on my running clothes.

I'll go sit with him and stretch and not say a word so he'll know how pissed I am, I thought. Real adult. God forbid I actually *talk* about how I'm feeling.

I went downstairs and found him sitting on the steps to the water, smoking (naturally), and I plopped down next to him and started stretching my right hamstring.

"What? Jogging?" he asked.

I hate it when people say I jog. I don't jog; I run. But I'd deal with that later. "Yep." I didn't look at him. *I'll show him!*

I kept stretching, and he kept smoking.

"Nice day," he said.

I took that as my cue to launch into it. "You were kind of an asshole last night."

"What do you mean?" he asked, confused.

I sighed. "I mean starting and then stopping. I told you I couldn't sleep if you did that. Why start it if you're not going to finish?"

"I am sorry," he said. "But that is the bed that my ex and I have slept in for years. When I thought about that, it hurt too much to keep going."

I wanted to point out that she was a lying, stealing bitch, but it didn't seem like the time for that. So I gave him an "I'm sorry" shoulder pat, said I'd be back in about an hour, and ran the two miles to the airport to check on my plane and pick up the bag of snacks inside of it so we would have something to eat for breakfast.

As I made my way there, I saw tons of debris from the storm littering the street—not a good sign. I picked up my pace.

My relief when I saw my baby tied down all nice and snug, having weathered that nasty storm just fine, was palpable. Damn that distracting Magnum, P.I.–looking line guy, but bless him for tying down my plane! I got my bag of snacks from the plane then went inside to talk to the FBO owner and see what the weather was supposed to do that day.

There was another stationary low parked over the Bahamas.

In December. When the weather is supposed to always be perfect. I was stuck there for another day, with absolutely nothing to do and very little to eat. *Well, if I'm stuck here, I'm at least going to make the most of it,* I decided. So on my two-mile walk back to Alfredo's (I tried to run with the bag of food, but it didn't really work), I thought of a couple of things for us to do. One was to take the big inter-island ferry to Nassau for a day, just for something different. The other was to rent a car, if we could find one, and drive down to Governor's Harbour, a small settlement about halfway down the island.

When I shared my ideas with Alfredo, I could tell he wasn't crazy about either idea. But he played along. "The ferry for Nassau leaves every day at 4 p.m.," he said. "But I don't want to leave the house alone right now. What if my ex comes here when I'm gone? She will take everything!"

So our day was going to be based on if and when Crazy Ex showed up to get the rest of her stuff. If she came early, then maybe we could do something. If she didn't come until late, like she had the night before, then we couldn't do a damn thing. Or so Alfredo said. But I wasn't giving up so easily.

I tried to call the number listed in my pilot guide for car rental, but the call wouldn't go through. Alfredo said the only guy he knew who rented a car—*a* car, not multiple cars—said he needed a part that wasn't expected to arrive for a while. But after calling a few people, Alfredo finally tried the gas station, and they said they had a car. It was Saturday, and they were of course closed on Sunday—every place on the islands is—so we either had to return it that same night or not until Monday. They wanted a ridiculous amount of money, but if it meant not being stuck sitting around and doing nothing, I didn't care.

"Monday," I told Alfredo, and he relayed the message. Then he called a taxi to take me to the gas station to pick up the car.

"Will you get some more wine and cigarettes?" he asked. "This situation—the restaurant, my ex—is making me so miserable. I have decided that I will drink and smoke as much as I please until I leave on Wednesday."

He'd been doing a good job of that already, and I think he saw that I was thinking that.

"I do not smoke at all when I am at home," he said. "And I drink like normal there, not so much."

I had to wonder what "normal" meant to him—but the good thing, if you can call it that, is that he seemed to have built up a high tolerance. Even with all the liquor and beers I saw him drink throughout the day while we were hanging out, I never saw him drunk.

I arrived back at his place with all the cash I'd had on me gone but a smile on my face. We had a car! Now we could *do* something!

"Should we go for a ride?" I asked Alfredo, half expecting him to say no—Crazy Ex still hadn't come, and he seemed pretty determined to stay there until she did.

"Yes," he said. "Let's go." I guess he was tired of waiting, too.

I drove us around the nearby towns, dodging the car-swallowing-sized potholes that were everywhere. A lot of the "roads" weren't paved; those were even worse than the pothole-littered paved ones. And this is a lot coming from someone from New Orleans, where the local newspaper runs an annual readers' survey about the worst potholes and even a pothole decorating contest—a common part of life there.

While we were driving around, every time Alfredo saw someone he knew, which was everyone, he asked me to stop so he could get out and have a quick chat. This is a common island practice—one of the reasons the coconut telegraph works so well. I got used to slamming on the brakes when the car in front of me (the few times there was one) stopped suddenly so the driver could have a spontaneous chat with a friend on the side of the road.

We returned to Alfredo's for a lunch of leftover pasta from the night before. We were just finishing up when we both heard a noise outside. He looked up from his plate and past me, through the door. A look of unpleasant surprise crossed his face.

"Wait right here!" he said quickly, and he jumped up and hurried outside.

I turned around to see two guys getting out of a pickup truck. Alfredo intercepted them before they got to the front door. I couldn't hear them from where I was sitting, but they talked animatedly for a minute, and then he came back in alone.

"Who was that?" I asked.

"One of them is my ex's best friend," he explained. "I don't know the other one. They said they just wanted to see the place, but that guy has seen this place plenty of times since I built it three years ago. It was bullshit. Then they asked if they could come in for a beer. I said I didn't have any, and I told them to leave and not come back." He ended his retelling of the encounter with something else that made me laugh: "They know they shouldn't-a mess with me. I'm a fucking-a mobster!"

That night, Alfredo grilled steaks and I made pasta to prove to him that I could cook pasta (he didn't believe I could do it). I'm still not sure what he thought about the pasta I made that night. He watched over me like a hawk while I was cooking it —"But *how* are you going to cook it?" he kept asking. I didn't have much to work with and wanted to do something simple, so I decided on a little olive oil, some herbs, and some parmesan cheese. I thought it was good. Alfredo didn't say anything, but he did eat it.

As we munched on Pop Tarts the next morning, we agreed to drive around the island and then fly if the weather looked good.

Our first stop was at a resort called The Cove, which was just north of the small town of Hatchet Bay. If someone had asked me to design my own island paradise, I think it would look a lot like The Cove. It sat in a remote area of the island in the middle of the most lush, healthiest-looking greenery I'd ever seen, and it was on a small hill, so it had absolutely breath-taking views of the flora and water below. A hammock tied between two trees outside was so postcard-perfect it looked fake. I wanted to get in it and never leave!

Looking down from the hammock, I had a view of a gorgeous deep turquoise cove, a private beach, and a few small thatched umbrellas. There was also a colorful wooden sign that pointed the way to the major islands in the Bahamas, each wooden arrow painted a different color. Nothing else I had seen on the trip so far could come close to this. Alfredo chatted with his friends while I soaked it all in, awe-struck.

"Are you ready to leave?" Alfredo asked when we'd been there for an hour or so.

"I guess so ..." I said reluctantly. I didn't want to leave, but I did want to know what other beauty on the island was in store for us.

Alfredo drank a beer as he drove us to our next destination —yet another laughable island occurrence that would never fly in the States but that I saw often while I was there (in pretty much every car we drove past, in fact). I normally wouldn't be okay with something like that, but when in Rome ...

The next stop on our drive was Cocodimama resort, owned

by some Italians Alfredo knew. He chatted with them in Italian and then introduced me, telling everyone at the bar that I was a pilot and had flown there from New Orleans. I felt like Amelia Earhart when everyone started bombarding me with questions, fascinated that a woman would fly alone so far away from home.

"She's taking me up in her plane later today," Alfredo boasted.

"Will you fly past the hotel later?" the bartender asked, brightening.

I can never resist a good flyby. "Of course!" I said.

"But how will I know it's you?" he asked.

"Oh you'll know," I replied, already plotting something of a private airshow for the hotel guests.

Since the weather was still very pleasant and mostly clear after we had lunch at Cocodimama, we decided it was time to take that flight we'd been talking about for days. We headed back up toward North Eleuthera Airport.

Hitching rides is very common on the islands, so I didn't mind when Alfredo stopped to pick up two men on our way to the airport—especially because they were very old men!

"Thank you, thank you!" they said as they climbed into the backseat. Their church, the only civilization around, had just finished Sunday service. It was a good fifteen miles back to the intersection in town where we dropped them off.

"How did you get here?" I asked. "Did someone give you a ride?"

"Oh no," one said. "We walked."

"All this way?" I asked, incredulous.

"We have to get up very early to get to the services on time, but it's not so bad walking in the morning," he responded. "But now with the midday heat setting in ... we're grateful for the ride!"

Wow, I thought. *These people take their churchgoing seriously!*

After dropping off the hitchhikers at the only corner in town, we drove to the airport. As I preflighted the airplane, I told Alfredo what I was checking, how things worked, and how things were connected, and tried to make him feel at ease by helping him understand how airplanes worked. He kept saying "Holy shit"—or rather, "Oly shee"—but I couldn't tell if he was really scared, or if he was excited about the flight, or if he was just joking around. Maybe it was all three.

To my delight, though, Alfredo seemed totally at ease once we got in the air. As soon as we were in the air, his face was plastered to the window like a kid on his first airplane ride, and he kept saying "Wow!" I wasn't sure at first if that was because he was scared or because he couldn't believe how beautiful it was, but I kept looking at his face and seeing a smile on it, so I figured it was the latter.

I knew the highlight for him would be flying over his friends' resort, so I decided to make it special. When we started getting close, I slowed the plane down, put in some flaps so I could keep a low power setting, and took us down to 100 feet over the water, just off Cocodimama's private beach. I waited until we were just abeam the resort and then added full power to give them some good audio and climbed the airplane out steeply. That would ensure they knew it was us! I turned 180 degrees over the adjacent cove, and I went back down to 200 feet as we passed the resort and rocked the wings to make the airplane wave at them.

I was glued to the cockpit instruments, making sure everything was functioning properly as we flew so low, so I wasn't looking at the hotel. But Alfredo was delighted. "There is a group of people on the terrace jumping and waving at us," he said. "They love it!"

We headed back to the airport after that. Alfredo was still plastered to the window, enjoying the scenery, the whole way back. Once I landed and parked the plane, he said he'd wait for me by the car while I gathered my flight gear, and I saw him light up a cigarette as soon as he was away from the ramp. The cigarette told me he was still a bit nervous about the flight, but he was also smiling. I was happy to be the first pilot to take him up in a small airplane.

I was sad to see our perfect day coming to an end. But Alfredo wasn't done yet. It was still light out, and he wanted to drive to Bluff, a nearby town, to show me around.

A few minutes into the drive, I happened to mention that I really wanted to eat/drink some coconuts while I was on the islands. "I haven't found any yet," I said. "Do you know where we can get some?"

Immediately, Alfredo started asking everyone we passed on the street where we could get some coconuts. Then he spotted a convenience store. He pulled over. "Let's try in there."

An elderly woman was manning the counter inside.

"Do you have coconuts?" Alfredo asked.

"I have a dry coconut but no jelly coconuts," she responded.

"Oh, is there more than one kind of coconut?" I said. I thought a coconut was a coconut.

She looked at Alfredo as if to ask "Where the hell did you find this clueless one?" She had the good grace not to say it out loud, however. Instead, she simply said, "Jelly coconuts are the only ones that have coconut water. You can't drink from dry coconuts."

Well that made sense, but what made one dry and one jelly? Not wanting to look stupid, I didn't ask—but I made a mental note to look it up later.

Not far from the convenience store, we stopped at a small dive bar on a shell road among some small houses. Clothes drying on lines zigzagged between trees. The setting was so bleak that I wondered why anyone would go there to drown their sorrows. A place like that would only make a bad mood worse. But we were there, and we were thirsty, so Alfredo ordered a beer and I a Sprite, and we sat outside to enjoy the breeze.

A bunch of locals were gathered on the other side of the street, drinking beer and barbecuing.

"What is the occasion?" Alfredo called out to one of them.

A man broke off from the group and walked over. After introducing himself as "Peter the fisherman," he said proudly, "My daughter was baptized today."

"Congratulations!" Alfredo said.

"You must join us!" he said. "Come say hello to my new friends!" he called out to the party, waving them over to us.

We didn't need much convincing—and since Peter the fisherman brought the party to us, we didn't exactly have a choice, either. For the next couple of hours, Peter's family treated us like best friends. At a certain point we met Rosy, a drunk and very outgoing socialite from the nearby island of Exuma. With the festivities, I had totally forgotten about wanting coconuts, but Alfredo hadn't.

"Do you know where we can get some coconuts?" he asked her. "Erin would like to try one."

"How many do you want?" Rosy asked immediately, turning to me.

"I dunno," I said, shrugging. "Maybe two, so we can each drink one?"

She made a beeline for a small group of men drinking beers a few yards away, and started gesturing and saying something I couldn't understand. Within minutes, they had all piled into a van and driven off.

While we were waiting for the coconuts and once again sitting alone—the party had moved back across the street—a teenage boy walked up and nodded to Alfredo shyly. In a second, I could see why he was so shy: he was physically challenged in some way. He had a twisted facial expression, and a bit of drool on his chin.

"How are you?" Alfredo asked.

The boy just nodded.

"Wipe your chin," Alfredo said gently, "and go inside the bar and get a soda on my tab. Okay?"

The boy's eyes lit up and he ran inside. He came out clutching a Sprite in his hands, a grin on his face.

I was impressed by Alfredo's humanity and small gesture of kindness. Most people would have ignored the boy; Alfredo acknowledged him and gave him something that cost him little, but was clearly a big deal to the boy.

About twenty minutes later, the minivan returned. Out piled Rosy and her entourage—with eight coconuts in hand.

"Amazing!" I said. "How much do I owe you?"

"Ten dollars," she said.

I gave her a twenty-dollar bill. Very resourceful girl, that Rosy. Coconuts delivered on demand!

Before I had time to wonder how we were going to drink said coconuts, a local took one out of my hand, masterfully chopped at it with a rusty machete, and handed it back to me without saying a word, a perfect little hole cut into its side. He cut one for Alfredo, too, and we clinked them together to toast our perfect island day.

IT WAS QUITE DARK WHEN WE PULLED UP TO THE SIDE of Alfredo's house and I walked up the back porch. I was the first through the door; the place was totally empty except for my luggage on the floor and Alfredo's few items. *Great.* Not the perfect end to our day that I was hoping for. In fact, it broke my heart that our day would end like this.

I walked back outside and met Alfredo as he approached the porch. "It's all gone," I said sadly. "She came while we were out."

He walked in to take a look. All the tables and chairs were gone from what was to be the dining area of the restaurant. She had also taken the refrigerator, leaving the food we'd had in it out on the countertop to spoil. It had already attracted a veritable parade of ants.

She did, in fact, leave all that was not hers. The problem was, almost everything was hers. It was also abundantly clear that she had emptied out my bags—probably to make sure I wasn't hiding anything of hers in them—and then repacked them. I was pretty upset that she'd gone through my things—I'd assumed that if she came by, she'd understand that the luggage was neither hers nor Alfredo's and ignore it—but I decided to let it go. There was nothing I could do about it. And Alfredo was upset enough as it was.

Alfredo wandered through the house, cataloguing his losses. The only thing he commented on was the fact that his expensive Italian suit was on the floor, but I could tell by his tone that he was still upset about the breakup. It hurt me to see how much this woman, who had wronged him in so many ways, was still hurting him. I wished I could say or do something to make him feel better, but there didn't seem to be anything to say. I hoped that just keeping him company would help.

Since we had nothing to eat and nothing to sleep on (the

mattress was hers too), I suggested that we go back to Cocodimama to spend the night. There were a few places a little closer than that, but I figured Alfredo would be happier there with his friends. It was just over an hour's drive away, and we were very tired from our long day, but it felt worth it.

"It's our last night together," I said. "Let's make it count."

He smiled. "Okay. Cocodimama it is."

I realized that this experience was beginning to mean a lot to me. I wasn't falling in love with Alfredo—I'd only known him a few days—but how could I share such a totally bizarre and fun five days with him and not get slightly attached?

As soon as we walked into Cocodimama, the bartender ran over.

"It was so cool when you flew by earlier!" he exclaimed. And that was just the beginning of what felt like a hero's welcome. All the guests in the bar talked about the flyby with the same fascination and excitement, as if it were the first time they had seen an airplane. Both Alfredo and I ate up the attention; it couldn't have come at a better time.

It was difficult to leave the bar—the questions just kept coming, and I could have drunk myself into a stupor with all of the drinks they offered us—but we finally made our way to our room and crawled into bed. I put my head on Alfredo's chest and breathed in his combination of cologne and cigarette smell. *Why is it that this is okay on him when it would be absolutely unacceptable on anyone else?* I wondered. I decided not to question it too much.

We had spectacularly delicious sex—so good that not even Alfredo's snoring could put me in a bad mood afterward. And I knew that would make it even harder to leave the next day. But it was time for me to fly on ... solo.

eighteen | GREAT
ABACO,
ELBOW KEY, AND
A LITTLE LONELINESS

*"You have brains in your head. You have feet in your shoes.
You can steer yourself any direction you choose."*
—DR. SEUSS, OH, THE PLACES YOU'LL GO!

I WOKE UP A BIT SAD, KNOWING THAT IT WAS time to say goodbye. Sure, I could stay until Alfredo left for home, but this trip was not about meeting men; it was about flying and exploring—going wherever the weather took me and my plane.

"I'd like to see you again," I told Alfredo as we drove to the airport. "Next time in the real world—or at least somewhere between the real world and this world!" I remembered his warning on the first night we spent together, and added, "I've really started to care for you—not *love* you, but care for you!"

We both laughed and he said, "I feel the same way."

I didn't pursue the conversation any further; I didn't want to get emotional. The weather was looking worse and worse, and it had even begun to rain a little. Time to get going, or I might never leave. So I packed my luggage in the airplane, did my preflight inspection, and checked the weather again on a computer in the FBO. It looked marginal getting out of Eleuthera, but it was clear in Marsh Harbour, Great Abaco, which was where I was headed. I decided to chance the iffy weather and leave. I didn't want to have to go through the emotional back and forth of leaving/not leaving as the weather changed.

Alfredo walked out to the plane with me. I had thought about what to say, but all that came out was, "Call me."

We hugged, and he kissed my neck and cheek. He said he'd wait in the car until I left.

I could see him parked on the side of the road as I started the airplane and did the pre-takeoff checks. I opened up the window and stuck my hand out to wave goodbye as I taxied to the runway. He was gone by the time I came rolling back down the runway on takeoff.

I wasn't all that sad as I departed Eleuthera because it wasn't at all clear that I was going to be able to continue on. The weather continued to threaten to turn until I was pretty close to Abaco, so for much of the flight I still felt there was a possibility I'd have to go back. I fantasized about how I would call Alfredo when I landed and ask him to come get me—how we'd get to spend at least one more night together. But the weather held, and once it was clear that I would indeed continue to Abaco—that Eleuthera was behind me once and for all —I started to get a little choked up.

It helped that Marsh Harbour, a town and airport on the island of Great Abaco, was clear and sunny. After going through the now-expected "Just you?" and "Who's the pilot?" questions at customs, I hopped a taxi to the dock, where I hopped a ferry to Elbow Cay, where I hopped a van to my hotel. The planes, trains, and automobiles thing was beginning to wear on me—figuring out the logistics of it all was mentally exhausting! Well ... all but the plane part. I could never tire of that.

GREAT ABACO IS ONE OF THE TOP SAILING DESTINATIONS in the world, and it showed: it seemed like everyone there had come in on a boat except me. I had decided to begin my stay there on Elbow Cay, one of the barrier islands, because Marsh Harbour had too much of a touristy city feel for my taste.

Elbow Cay (pronounced "key"), one of many in a chain of cays off Great Abaco's eastern shore, is about six miles long and a quarter mile wide. The main town there, Hope Town, was settled by British loyalists seeking refuge during the eighteenth century, after the American Revolution. As the water taxi pulled into the harbor, I could see the cay's famous candy-striped lighthouse. It's one of the last operational kerosene-fueled lighthouses in the world, and was apparently rather controversial when built because many islanders made their living by salvaging ships that wrecked on the surrounding reefs—they knew the lighthouse would improve navigation and eventually put them out of business.

I had decided to stay at the Abaco Inn because it offered a pilot discount, and my vacation money was quickly running out. As the hotel van driver explained to me on the way, the hotel was designed totally "island style" and therefore had no locks on the doors. I thought I had misheard him, but he was right. There was a sliding glass door, but no lock. There was a dowel that I could use as a lock when I was *in* the room, which made me feel safer at night, but it didn't help for when I wanted to leave the room and keep my luggage safe. The van driver had explained to me that there was no crime on Elbow Cay—"We only have one policeman here, and all he does is eat, sleep, and shit, if you'll excuse my language"—but I couldn't help but worry a little bit. I had heard about how the criminals that generally frequented Nassau, where most of the tourists go, occasionally came "down island" to commit crimes away from any police, so it wasn't like it was 100 percent safe. And who was to say that the other visitors there weren't criminals? Maybe the Bahamians on the whole behaved themselves, but what about the other travelers?

I stayed for two nights so I could explore the town and shop a little. Elbow Cay really was more like what I had pictured all the islands would look like: there were cute little Victorian houses painted in bright colors with intricate lattice-work, sidewalks and walkways with no cars, and a mix of natives and expats. As hard as it had been to leave Alfredo, I was glad I was giving myself a chance to see more of the islands. That was the point of the trip in the first place, right?

nineteen | ALMOST
BUSTED FLAT
IN
GRAND BAHAMA

"Tourists don't know where they've been,
travelers don't know where they're going."
—PAUL THEROUX

     HAD TO BE BACK TO WORK EARLY ON MONDAY,
so by midweek I had to start thinking about getting
back home. Normally I could make the flight back
home in one day, with a stop or two for fuel along the way, but I
had to factor in the weather, which was looking iffy yet again. I
had planned to fly straight to Florida, passing over Grand Bahama
along the way, but now I wasn't sure if that was possible.

  I took the 9:45 a.m. ferry from Hope Town on Elbow Cay to
Marsh Harbour. When I got there, I found that—even though I
had asked them to—they hadn't fueled up the plane yet. They
said they were waiting to hear from the owner of the plane. I
had told them I was the owner, but I guess, like all the customs
officers, they didn't believe me.

  While I was waiting for them to fill up the tank, I used the
pilot courtesy phone to inquire about the weather. There was a

big front over Florida; there was no way I could make it there VFR. Begrudgingly, I decided to amend my trip and at least get to Freeport, Grand Bahama, the next island to the west and the closest one to Florida. I'd wait out the weather there so I could be ready to head home when it cleared. It would be about an hour flight from Marsh Harbour, and even that was starting to look marginal.

The flight from Marsh Harbour to Freeport was about the only flight I made during my entire time in the Bahamas where I didn't have to keep getting lower and lower due to weather. I could see the front coming from the west, and I made it to the Freeport Airport a few hours before the low cloud ceiling arrived and stayed for days.

Grand Bahama is the fifth-largest island in the Bahamas— about ninety-three miles long, and twelve miles wide at its widest point. Like many of the other islands, Grand Bahama was once home to the Lucayan Indians. Later, it was resettled by former slaves after the British Empire abolished slavery. It then became a smuggling port for runners supplying goods to the Confederacy during the American Civil War and then again for rum-runners during Prohibition. Today, Freeport serves as a commercial ship harbor and is home to Grand Bahama's main airport.

Freeport had an actual control tower, unlike the other island airports I had been to, but it was non-radar, meaning they had nothing to show them where I was in the air, so the tower controller told me to report when I was twenty-five miles out, and then again when I was downwind in the traffic pattern. I heard that mysterious radio noise again as I approached— more this time than I had on any previous legs of the trip—and this time it was so bad that I couldn't hear the controller when I got close to Freeport, and I had to ask him to "say again" multiple times.

Just when I was about to switch to a headset I always carry as a backup, the noise stopped. *Weird.* Nothing to do about it now, but I was determined to figure out what the problem was when I returned home. It made me nervous to not be able to hear radio transmissions.

I cleared customs—this time without the usual "It's just you?" or "You're the pilot?" questions, to my great surprise—and took a taxi to the Pelican Bay Hotel at Taino Beach in the town of Lucaya, the sister city to Freeport. I was glad to see that the roads had wide, grassy shoulders in both directions, perfect for running, since it looked like I'd be stuck here for a few days.

Once I got settled into my first-floor hotel room right on a marina, I went for a run back down the main road, which led to the Port Lucaya Marketplace. I was a little disappointed by what I saw: it was a pretty island, but there was nothing around Lucaya for miles. And that included restaurants. Back at the hotel, I asked the concierge where I could get something to eat.

"You'll have to go into Port Lucaya," she said, and that was it.

"How ..." I started to ask, but I could already see that she was too indifferent to be of any help whatsoever. *Why bother?*

I walked outside and saw two women about to get into a taxi at a neighboring hotel.

"Are you headed to Port Lucaya?" I called out to them, anxious to share the fare.

They didn't answer me—in fact, they didn't even turn their heads. They jumped in, and the taxi pulled away.

I was beginning to feel frustrated. I looked around. Another lady was off to my right, standing under the drop-off awning of the hotel entryway.

"Are *you* headed to Port Lucaya?" I asked.

"Yes, but a friend is coming to pick me up," she said.

I sighed. *Of course.*

"Why don't you take the ferry?" she suggested. "It's cheaper than taking a cab."

I brightened a little bit. "Where can I catch it?"

She pointed back down the street to my hotel. "Just behind that hotel."

The concierge couldn't have given me that information?

"It leaves every hour on the hour," the helpful lady volunteered.

"Thanks so much," I said, and with a wave, I walked back to my hotel—where I found the small ferry sitting just feet from the door to my room.

I had been sitting on the ferry with a few other people for about ten minutes, waiting for it to leave, when a girl ran up.

"Will you wait for my boyfriend?" she pleaded, one foot on the ferry and one on land. "He's almost here!"

The ferry operator shrugged noncommittally.

At a few minutes past the hour, just when the boyfriend was running down the dock, the operator started the engine and motored away, leaving them both stranded there. Nothing like extending a friendly gesture to make a good impression on visitors in a country that relies on tourism as its main source of income! The Bahamas tourism board always touts the islands as being full of hospitality, but clearly they hadn't seen some of the hospitality or transportation employees in action.

The ferry ride was beautifully romantic—the lights along the shore reflecting off the water—and made me really lonely. Luckily, it was only a five-minute ride.

We got dropped off in front of a restaurant in Port Lucaya. I had no idea what was there, so I followed the people who had been sitting next to me, figuring they'd lead me to ... whatever was there. We passed a couple of restaurants, and then I saw La Dolce Vita, and knew it was my destiny. If I was going to be missing the Italian, I figured I could at least enjoy some of his country's food.

The meal was actually one of the best I had on the trip. I was now at the point of the trip where I was watching every penny I spent—to make sure I'd have enough to get home—but I even splurged on a Kalik, the Bahamian beer of choice, which wears the slogan "It's a Bahamian ting" on its label.

"Is the chef Italian?" I asked when the waiter came to check on me partway through my meal. I was secretly hoping to meet another Italian man since my time with Alfredo had been so much fun.

"No, he's Bahamian," the waiter said. "He just loves Italian food!"

Damn.

I had some time before I needed to catch the ferry back to my hotel—even with planning to be a few minutes early—so I walked around the Port Lucaya Marketplace, one of the largest "straw markets" in the Bahamas, though I saw no straw for sale. The shops were all closed, but that wasn't too disappointing— I'd be there for a few days, waiting for the bad weather to pass. I'd have more time to walk around. The place looked a lot like Downtown Disney: it was a cute, colorful outdoor mall with overpriced shops and restaurants. Yes, I had struck tourist mecca— not my usual scene, but I still wanted to make the most of it.

THE NEXT DAY, I TOOK THE FERRY—SHOWING UP EARLY so as not to miss it—back to Port Lucaya to explore some more. I walked out to the lighthouse, hoping to take some pictures, but it was enclosed by a private resort's wall and didn't look like you could access it. By then it was late afternoon, and the surrounding resorts and expensive shops just didn't do anything for me, so I decided to have an early dinner and head back to my hotel.

I ate dinner in the outdoor mall—big mistake. The food was terrible, and so full of garlic that that's all I could taste. I wanted to stop at one of the convenience stores to buy a big bottle of water (and perhaps some mints?) to keep in my hotel before catching the ferry back, but the service was so slow at the restaurant that I started to get nervous that I would miss the ferry.

Check finally paid, I checked my watch: fifteen minutes to go. I really wanted that water. I power-walked to the store and bought a big bottle (alas, they didn't have any mints), then made a beeline for the ferry.

I should have known better than to cut the timing so close. As I neared the marina, I saw the boat at the dock, and I knew I didn't have much time, even though it was 8:08 p.m. and it wasn't supposed to leave until 8:15. I ran. I know the ferry driver saw me; I was right in his line of vision. But he pulled away before I got there anyway.

This one guy was doing a great job of ruining the friendly image of the islands, and he seemed to take pleasure in doing so. I was stuck waiting another hour for the next ferry—and of course, this was when it started to blow outside like a hurricane was coming.

I was stuck in my hotel room staring through my sliding glass door at torrential rain for the next two days. Listening to the thunder cracking outside, I began to doubt if I'd make it home on Sunday. It was already Saturday, and I had about eight or nine hours of flying in order to get back home. There were numerous reports of moderate to severe turbulence over Florida and a strong headwind. But the front had technically passed. It was not going to be fun flying, but the conditions weren't necessarily dangerous. I made a decision: I had to get home. If it were even remotely possible, I would leave the next morning.

 *twenty* | ANOTHER
LONG
JOURNEY HOME

"A ship is safe in the harbor, but that's not what ships are built for."
—GAEL ATTAL

I WAS THE FIRST ONE TO ARRIVE AT CUSTOMS AT Freeport Airport that morning—as in, not even the customs officers were there yet. The office was supposed to open at 9 a.m., but the first officer didn't mosey in till around nine fifteen, at which point she chatted with all the other office staff before helping anyone in line.

I had already paid my ten-dollar landing fee and fifteen-dollar departure tax; all that was left was to fill out the forms on the desk before me. I got it done as quickly as possible and returned them to the customs officer, who looked at all the stamps from the different islands I had been to and said, "You've been all over the world!"

"Well, all over the Bahamas, at least," I said. She was clearly impressed. But I had barely even made a dent in the list of islands I wanted to go to.

"Most pilots who fly over just pick one island and park it there," she said. Then she launched into the "It's just you traveling alone?" and "Were you meeting someone here?" questions. That made it consistent on all five islands I flew to. And here I'd thought Grand Bahama would be the exception.

I took off in the worst crosswind I'd ever experienced. Once airborne, I had to do a 45-degree crab angle into the wind to stay flying in line with the runway. The flight itself—to Fort Pierce, Florida, where I was to clear customs—wasn't too bumpy, but I had a twenty-five-knot headwind slowing me way the hell down. I found myself looking straight down every minute or so just to verify that I was actually moving at all.

Because I was moving so slowly, I had plenty of time to think and look at my map during the flight—and that's when I realized something weird: that mysterious radio noise I had been getting on and off during the trip had started when I entered the Bermuda Triangle, and now that I had flown out of it, it had stopped. I really don't believe in all the stories about the Bermuda Triangle, but there must at the very least be some odd magnetic interference there that causes radio malfunctions. Even my fancy, fully functioning GPS lost its position for a few minutes just before I exited the Triangle. It was the first time it had ever done that, and it has never done it since. Cue the *Twilight Zone* music.

Just as I was freaking myself out with thoughts of scrambled airwaves and disappeared planes, the shoreline of Florida and the Fort Pierce Airport came into sight—and then the turbulence started. It was terrible by the time I landed; as I taxied down the runway, I was thankful to be on the ground—not a familiar sentiment for me!

I shut down the engine and opened the door to say hi to the line guy who approached the plane.

"Do you need customs?" he asked.

I nodded. "Yes please!"

"Okay," he said. "Stay in your plane and I'll tow you back to customs."

I looked back over my shoulder. We were nearly in front of the customs building, but apparently you had to park *right* in front.

The line guy towed me back the twenty feet and came back around. "Just stay in the plane until a customs officer comes out, okay?" he called out.

I didn't have to wait long; an officer came out a minute later. He climbed in, looked all around the plane for a few minutes, and then said, "You can get out, pilot."

I climbed out and chatted with him for a minute about where I had come from, and he told me to unload everything except my maps and to come into the building so my stuff could be processed.

Everything? I thought, taking stock of all my things. After all the shopping and shell and coconut collecting I had done, I was coming back with a whole lot more than I'd left with. Nonetheless, I loaded up two luggage carts while the line guy, who couldn't offer help since I hadn't cleared customs yet, watched with amusement.

I dragged my overflowing carts unsteadily inside, the coconuts rolling off right and left. I felt like a Bahamian luggage cart version of the Clampetts and was highly amused about what I must look like.

I waited in line and handed my passport to the customs officer when it was my turn. He swiped my passport, checked the computer, gave me a once-over to compare me to my passport picture, and said, "Go through that back door there." He pointed to where I had come in.

Are we done? I wondered. His words hadn't exactly made it clear if the process was over and I could take my luggage with me or if there would be, like, armed guards waiting for me outside.

"You don't need to go through any of my stuff?" I asked, hovering there.

"I *said*, go through that back door there," he said, visibly annoyed.

Right. You don't have to tell me three times! I walked out thinking of all the contraband I could have brought in had I known he wouldn't even search my luggage. Later, when I told my friends how lax they had been, they all claimed dibs on Cuban cigars for next time.

I repacked the airplane, trying to remember where I had so carefully placed everything before so the plane was evenly weighted, then refueled and took off into yet another roaring crosswind. I hit huge bumps the second I was airborne. I also found myself up against a thirty-knot headwind once I turned more northwesterly—which, unfortunately, was the direction I needed to go in. The turbulence was so bad that my stomach was instantly unhappy. I'd gotten used to the occasional choppy turbulence, the kind that feels almost rhythmic, but this was the kind that sent stuff into the air if it wasn't anchored down. I could hear the airplane creaking every time the turbulence forced it to flex. I knew I wouldn't last very long and didn't want to get to the point that I was disoriented from dizziness, so I kept my gaze focused on the horizon in the distance to minimize the movement my brain had to process.

I usually fly at about 120 knots, and I was making only 90, which felt excruciatingly slow. After flying in the relentless turbulence for three hours—hard flying with constant control inputs and throttle changes to deal with the rough air outside—I couldn't take it anymore. I saw a small airport out my right window and checked the map to see where I was. Cross City, Florida.

Suck it up and at least make it to Tallahassee, Erin, I told myself. The hotel I'd stayed in there on the way to Bimini had been nice. But at the speed I was going, it would be another hour before I got to Tallahassee, and I was beginning to get airsick! Cross City Airport, sitting right outside my window, was just too tempting. I called Jacksonville approach control on the radio and told them to amend my destination to Cross City.

"I've had two recent reports that the turbulence lightens up a bit past Tallahassee," the controller said helpfully.

There was no way I could stand another hour of that beating. "Thanks and it's tempting, but I'm not gonna make it that far. Cross City, please," I said firmly.

When I landed, I called home briefly, and then sat in the airplane, burping—getting out all the gas the turbulence had churned up in my stomach. After the burping subsided, I took out my luggage and walked to the FBO.

"Any suggestions for where I should stay?" I asked the elderly attendant, who identified himself as Don.

"There are only a few small hotels in town," he said, scratching his head. "I'd suggest the Carriage Inn. Nice lady runs it. And you can take the crew car overnight, if you like."

I drove the half mile to the Carriage Inn and was greeted by a friendly older lady with an accent I recognized as Polish.

"Don from the airport sent me," I told her after our initial greeting.

"Are you a pilot?" she asked, looking confused.

"Yes," I responded simply.

"Oh!" she said, sounding surprised. "You're the first female pilot I've ever seen! Congratulations!"

I didn't really know how to respond to that. "Uh ... thanks!" I managed.

"Your airplane, is it okay?" she asked.

"Yeah, it's fine," I said.

She must have noticed the befuddled expression on my face. "Most people who stop in Cross City are here because something is broken," she explained.

Makes sense, I thought. *Not much else reason to come here!* What I said was, "Well, my plane is just fine. But the turbulence was so bad up there that I just wanted to wait it out and rest."

She nodded. "Well, here's your room key," she said, taking my fifty dollars (half of what I'd paid at even the cheapest places I'd stayed in over the past two weeks). "Enjoy your stay!"

Once I got to my room, I decided to face the thing I dread most about vacations: catch up on work e-mail. I likely wouldn't have time to do it the next day when I returned home, and given that there was nothing to do in this town, I didn't really have an excuse not to. I opened up my laptop. *Ouch.* I had 1,100 emails. It took me the entire day to get through them, minus the time it took me to put gas in the crew car and get dinner from the only restaurant in town, Hardee's.

Not the most fun way to end my vacation. But at least I'd gotten the annoying stuff out of the way. Now I'd be able to spend my time at home the next day focused on my other returning-from-vacation rituals: doing laundry, unpacking, and grocery shopping.

I LEFT THE HOTEL EARLY IN THE MORNING AND WENT straight to the airport. There were still reports of turbulence over Florida, from where I was to Tallahassee, but again it was supposed to get a little better west of Tallahassee. *Can I endure another three and a half hours of that?* I wasn't sure.

Don fueled up the plane while I waited in the warm FBO.

Being back in the cold winter was a shock to my system. I couldn't feel my fingers by the time I finished pre-flighting the plane. I took off between a bunch of crop dusters and headed west. To my relief, there was no turbulence, just haze so thick that I barely had a land/sky horizon reference. I was still dealing with a stiff headwind, but it was better than it had been the previous day.

The headwind abated as I flew into Alabama, so that I briefly got up to a blistering 112 knots—still not as fast as I was used to, but it felt damn good after the previous day's endless hours of plodding along at 88 knots. But the headwind started to pick up again in Louisiana, and my progress slowed. By the time my home airport was in sight, I was more than ready to be there.

My parents were waiting there for me when I landed, all smiles. I shivered in the unfamiliarly cold air while they helped me load the luggage cart that they had rolled out to the plane from the FBO. After just two weeks away, everything felt so foreign to me. The horns, revving engines, big airplanes flying over, and people surrounding us as my parents drove me back to my condo seemed extraordinarily loud to me—so much so that I was tempted to stick my fingers in my ears to block it all out. Coming back from vacation is always a bit of a shock, but this time was a doozy!

I spent the whole day reliving my vacation as I told my parents about it. I was so glad to be home, but I also missed the warmth and gentle breezes of the islands. Winter had not let up yet there in New Orleans, and the cold ran right through me. And there were so many cars everywhere! It felt like my brain needed to be rewired to home life.

ABOUT TEN MONTHS AFTER MY BAHAMAS TRIP, WHEN I hadn't heard from Alfredo at all (despite my having sent him a nice care package containing a copy of *Don't Stop the Carnival* and various New Orleans goodies like pralines and spices for him to cook with), I got an unexpected and out of the blue e-mail from him:

> "sorry I haven't written ... how are you? ... how's flying ... really enjoyed our time together and will never forget it ... restaurant project in Eleuthera on hold for now ... I love you too."

Too? When did I ever say "I love you" to him? "You've got to be kidding me!" I said out loud to my empty living room. I mean, ten months of radio silence, and suddenly he's all lovey-dovey? When he's the one who told me not to fall in love in the first place?

Men.

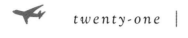 *twenty-one* | JOURNEY
TO MECCA

*"The whole object of travel is not to set foot on foreign land; it is at last
to set foot on one's own country as foreign land."*
—G. K. CHESTERTON

ONTINUING IN MY WORK HABIT OF GOING YEARS
without taking more than a few days of vacation here
and there, two and a half years passed after my journey
to the Bahamas without me taking a single long vacation. I was
still flying often, but only on short trips of an hour or two,
usually just to go someplace for lunch on the weekends. I was
definitely feeling the lack of adventure, and knew it was past
time to do something about it.

The problem was, I had lost my job during the worst part of
the recession of 2012, and career opportunities were virtually
nonexistent. It was clear that I'd be out of a job for a long time.
In a different situation, I would have welcomed the forced
break from work, since I always work 200 percent and often run
myself into the ground doing it, but with a healthy mortgage on
my beloved lake condo and my payments on Orion, I was eating
through my savings at an alarming rate. And I was becoming
more and more depressed over my bleak situation. I had called

every friend and former co-worker I could think of who might just know someone who knows someone who could help me find a job in this dismal market, to no avail. It was definitely not a good time to have a very niche skill set in the world of finance.

When you lose your job in the worst economy in American history, you have to find some way to look at the bright side. I decided it was finally time for my trip to Mecca. No, not Saudi Arabia—Oshkosh, Wisconsin. Confused? Well I guess I should clarify: I was looking to go to *Aviation* Mecca.

Oshkosh is home to the annual Experimental Aircraft Association (EAA) Airventure, a huge aviation gathering. It lasts a week, and during that week, the airport's control tower is the busiest in the world—some ten to fifteen thousand aircraft come and go during those seven days. That's a lot of airplanes to move around in a small area safely!

EAA estimates its actual number of attendees to be 300,000–500,000 people, making it not only the largest fly-in in terms of airplanes but also the most well-attended aviation gathering in the United States. How could anyone interested in aviation pass *that* up?

Well, despite the fact that I'd been dying to attend for a long time, I had never been able to go—because it was held in July, one of the busiest times of the year in my industry. For years I'd only been able to listen jealously as my friends who attended told tales of their experiences there. So when I lost my job in April and was still unemployed at the end of July, I felt it was written in the stars: after over eight years of flying without attending Airventure, it was time!

Mind you, since I was unemployed and had no idea when I *would* be employed, I was doing my best to keep all spending to a minimum. But I reasoned that this could be a once-in-a-lifetime chance for me. Who knew if my next job would allow me time off to attend in future years? If I were ever able to get a job again, it would probably be at another financial company, and I knew I would have the same too-busy time in July if that were the case. So I made a deal with myself: I would allow myself to spend money to fly there in my plane, camp in the "North 40" section of the airport—reserved for people pitching a tent under the wing of the airplane to get the full experience—and then fly back. I would do the trip as cheaply as possible, but I would do the trip.

Of course, just two weeks before Airventure, I get a bite from a company interested in hiring me right away. *But ... but ... Oshkosh!* I told them I was going out of town for five days at the end of July and asked if we could work around that, hoping that my desperation to go to Airventure wouldn't cost me this job I needed so badly. Luckily, my potential future boss was also a pilot and therefore totally understood when I 'fessed up to where I was going!

I asked a flight instructor friend, Joelle, if she wanted to come along. I wanted more than one set of eyes to look out for traffic as we arrived in the congested airspace—and a little company would be nice, too, of course. Flight instructors spend about 95 percent of their time in the traffic pattern of their home airport, so talking one into taking an actual cross-country flight is usually easy. Luckily for me, Joelle was no exception. She was more than happy to come along.

Then, as the event approached, the weather started to look like it wasn't going to cooperate.

Of course.

But ... but ... Oshkosh! I complained silently as I scanned the weather report. *Doesn't the universe get that I need to go to Oshkosh?!* Surely, I reasoned, the weather gods would take pity on me and offer clear skies. But the closer we got to go time, the less optimistic I was. There was a storm moving into Wisconsin and Illinois on the afternoon we were planning to arrive. The flight would take a little over seven hours, depending on the wind, but we also had to plan to arrive either before or after the daily airshow, which ran from 2:30 to 6:30 p.m., during which time the airport was closed to all arriving and departing traffic.

The original plan was to take our time getting up there, stop for a good BBQ lunch in Memphis, and arrive after the airshow but before eight, when the airport closed for the night. No problem—except for that damn storm!

The night before we left, I decided to switch up our plan: we would leave super early and skip lunch so we could hopefully arrive before the airshow and before the storm. We'd still have to stop once—to fuel up—so I picked the halfway point of Sikeston, Missouri. That would make each leg just around three and a half hours—which is about as long as my bladder can last anyway. Perfect.

Of course, with the weather threat running through my head and knowing I had to get up so early, I only slept for two hours. Not good! I become nearly non-functioning when I don't get enough sleep. But I was so excited to finally be going to Oshkosh when I got up the next morning that I knew I'd be okay for the flight. I just hoped we could take a nap once we got there.

We took off around 6:45 a.m. with sandwiches we'd packed for lunch and a bag of snacks in case we got stuck somewhere. It was quite hazy in the air, so there really wasn't much to see—disappointing, since I was looking forward to seeing a part of the country I'd never seen before. I'd flown my plane from San Francisco to New Orleans, and New Orleans to the Bahamas, but never straight north from Louisiana. *Oh well*, I thought. *Maybe on the way home.*

I flew the whole first leg as Joelle dozed. She only woke up when she heard air traffic control call my tail number—her flight instructor reflexes kicking in, I supposed. It was a pleasant, if unscenic, flight, and precisely at the three-and-a-half-hour mark, we landed in Sikeston.

One of the benefits of being a solo female pilot in a sea of male pilots is that I get a little special attention here and there. And when I'm with another woman, the chances of special treatment only increase. A bit chauvinist, perhaps, but I'm not above using it to my advantage at times! We gladly accepted the young (male) attendants' offer to pump our fuel while we went to the bathroom even though we had pulled up to the self-service pump. Once out of the bathroom, I paid for the fuel while Joelle checked the weather. We were back on the runway and heading out in about fifteen minutes ... some sort of record!

Joelle's weather check had revealed that the storm's progress east had slowed, which allowed me to relax a little; it meant that we should definitely be able to make it the whole way to Oshkosh in one day. Now we just had to beat the airshow or be stuck waiting somewhere else for four hours. We could just make it, but we had to be quick. Thanks to our expedited stop —and a tailwind—we were making good time to Oshkosh. It looked like we were going to make it.

With our timing figured out, I now had to focus on all the very specific instructions we needed to follow in order to arrive safely. I had already read the NOTAM (short for Notices to Airmen, which are issued when detailed information is needed about an airport or a navigational aid; I really wish they'd change the outdated FAA references to air*men*) twice, but there was a lot to remember. Normally NOTAMs are a few lines long; this one was thirty-two pages. I had written down the most important instructions on a Post-it note, knowing there'd be no way to page through the whole NOTAM while also flying my airplane. I figured I'd stick it to the yoke once we got close so I'd have it right in front of me.

The first arrival waypoint was a town called Ripon, and we were to arrive at Ripon at 1,800 feet and 90 knots. As we were getting close, I made the necessary adjustments to our altitude and speed. Now that I was down low on this windy, hot day it was pretty bumpy, so I was working all the controls to keep the plane at 1,800 and 90 knots! The instructions for Ripon were very strict: We were to listen to a specific frequency, but—unlike all other times when flying—we were ONLY to listen, not talk back, not even to acknowledge receipt of the controller's transmission. When they needed to be sure we heard them, the controllers would tell us to rock our wings. They were standing on a hillside so that they could clearly see all traffic.

If there were any planes in front of us when we arrived at Ripon, we were to maintain a distance of half a mile between our plane and the one in front of us. (I didn't have to worry about that one—there was no one immediately in front of us when we entered the airspace.) Once we got through Ripon, we were to follow train tracks leading northeast out of there to the next waypoint, another small town, Fisk.

We kept our eyes peeled for the train tracks and flew directly over them, though we had to point the airplane into the crosswind to fly straight over the tracks. The controllers in Ripon said nothing to us; I hoped that was because we were following the NOTAM and because there was no conflicting traffic.

As we approached Fisk, an air traffic controller gave us instructions on which dot on the runway was ours. Yep—a dot. Normally, only one plane is allowed on the runway at a time; they have to taxi completely clear of the runway before another plane can legally land. But because of the high volume of traffic at Airventure, the FAA issues the EAA a waiver for reduced runway spacing for landing, making it possible for three planes to land more or less simultaneously. To make it easy visually, rather than saying "Land 1,500 feet behind the plane in front of you," there are three colored dots—each one 1,500 feet apart, in accordance with the FAA's requirements—painted on the 6,000-foot runway.

This system was entirely foreign to me; I was used to knowing I had the entire runway to myself. But I tried not to psych myself out. *As long as I and all the other pilots follow the instructions from air traffic control,* I thought, *things will go off without a hitch.*

The NOTAM said to expect instructions from the air traffic controller on the ground before we hit Fisk, but we were getting close, and I hadn't heard anything yet.

"Do you think they missed us?" I asked Joelle—but before she could answer, I heard, "Cessna three-quarters of a mile from Fisk, rock your wings."

Ah! I had waited so long to hear that! I rocked my wings.

"Good rock, Cessna," the controller said. "Proceed on a right downwind for runway 27, turn base inside the gravel pit."

I hoped the gravel pit would be readily apparent. I did not want to be "that pilot" who screwed everything up, especially since one of my air traffic controller friends from Louis Armstrong International was controlling at Oshkosh for the week and I didn't want to embarrass myself in front of him! But I needn't have worried—the gravel pit was huge and hard to miss once we could see it.

Just as I started my turn, the controller said, "Cessna inside the gravel pit, cleared to land green dot runway 27 behind a jet on a two-mile final."

I immediately saw the jet and extended my downwind leg just a little to give myself enough room to avoid his wake turbulence.

"No, Cessna, keep your turn coming," the controller broke in. "Aim straight for the green dot."

I did what I was told, but seconds later, the controller backtracked. "Sorry about that, Cessna, that's not going to work. Cessna, go around and re-enter right downwind for runway 27. I swear I won't send you around again."

I powered up and retracted the flaps to go around and climbed out to re-enter the pattern. Once I was on downwind, the controller said, "Sorry about that, Cessna. You are now cleared to land green dot runway 27. Aim straight for the green dot now."

I had just barely passed the green dot on the downwind leg, so this was going to be a tight pattern and wouldn't allow me much time to stabilize the final approach. And since it was still windy and bumpy, trying to maintain the right approach angle to the green dot meant that my right hand was in and out with the throttle lever while my left hand was up and down with the yoke—tricky stuff.

The controller saw me struggling, and he got nervous. "Cessna, you can't land before the green dot. I have someone landing behind you on the orange dot. Don't land before the green dot."

I'M NOT! I wanted to say back to him, but since we couldn't talk back, I couldn't say anything. So I settled for complaining silently, in my head: *Just let me do my thing!* And I did do my thing: I plopped Orion RIGHT DOWN on the green dot! I was proud of myself for doing that after such a crazy few minutes. *Take that, controller!* I thought, feeling smug.

And then he said those three immortal words that every

pilot longs to hear—"Welcome to Oshkosh"—and all was forgiven.

The instructions said to turn off of the runway as soon as possible after landing, so I immediately turned left onto the bumpy grass. There were flaggers standing at fifty-foot intervals, since planes could turn off the runway at any point, and the one closest to me started to flag me towards him, then pointed to the plane that had just landed behind me on the orange dot and signaled for him to hold while I pulled in front of him, and then pointed to me and signaled for me to hold for another plane that had just landed and pulled off in front of me! The amount of traffic there was mind-boggling. But the controllers and the volunteer flaggers were handling it all expertly, turning chaos into organization.

The NOTAM had warned us to prepare signs to put in our window identifying where we wanted to park so the flaggers would know where to send us on the immense airport field. Mine read "GAC," short for "general aviation camping." The flaggers pointed me straight ahead to follow a long line of cones they had set up as a makeshift taxiway. With all the planes taxiing in line in front of and behind me, I felt like a jet in rush hour traffic at LAX.

I knew we were getting close when I saw hundreds of planes lined up in rows with tents pitched under their wings. We were directed up a row, turned 90 degrees, and finally signaled to shut down the engine. Three flaggers were on hand to help us push the plane straight back into what would be our parking and camping space for the next three nights. They were also very helpful with telling us where to go to register, eat, and use bathrooms with flush toilets (as opposed to the porta-potties scattered around the field).

Finally, I thought, taking it all in. After years of dreaming about going, I had arrived at Oshkosh and the famous North 40 camping! And it sure looked like heaven to me! Airplanes of all kinds as far as the eye could see in every direction.

Now to secure the plane and pitch the tent. We had three two-foot-long steel tie-down anchors that screwed into the ground and had a loop at the top to tie a rope from it to each wing and the tail. But since we had never used them before, we hadn't thought ahead of time about *how* we would screw them into the ground. Whoops.

After seeing that there was no way we could do it by hand, we pulled the metal tow bar from the baggage compartment in the plane. It had a handle that we put through the tie-down loop, and still it took all our strength to turn it and push it into the ground. Within seconds of that effort, we were sweating our guts out. With the two of us taking turns, it was about an hour before we had all three screwed into the ground and the airplane tied to them.

My controller friend—callsign "Porkchop," because he's a big, strong guy—arrived just as we were finishing the job. Nice timing! Still, we put him to use helping to pitch the tent. I had camped a grand total of two times before in my life, and both times were in what most people would consider "luxury" camp-ground accommodations—like one of those times was in a Disney World campground. (I, myself, believe that "luxury campground" is an oxymoron. But perhaps that's just me.) Both of my camping experiences had also been with a friend who camped all the time and had pitched the tent without me lifting a finger or even paying attention. Which was proving to be a problem now. I had no idea where to even begin.

At the beginning, I guess, I thought, so I slid the tent—bor-rowed from a friend rather than purchased, since I knew damn well I'd never use it again—out of its bag and laid the pieces out on the ground. It looked to me like a random collection of metal rods and pieces of cloth. I searched for a set of instructions, to no avail. Then I looked at Joelle and Porkchop.

"You guys have any idea what to do with this thing?"

They laughed. "Why don't you just unload the airplane," Joelle suggested, "and we'll get this set up."

"Deal!" I walked away wondering why they don't just have self-erecting tents—you know, like those air beds that blow themselves up when you plug them in. Genius, right? Anyway. I busied myself with unloading the airplane while the other two toiled with the tent. Once it was up, I helped them stake it into the ground and then put our sleeping bags and luggage inside. At which point I noticed just how small it was.

"Um ..." I said out loud, scratching my head. This tent was allegedly a four-person tent, but our two sleeping bags and two very small suitcases pretty much filled it up. *This thing could only fit four people if they were packed like sardines with overlapping body parts*, I thought. But no bother. I'd worry about the details later, when we actually had to get in it—which I wasn't going to do until it was absolutely necessary.

"Do you guys want to come check out the control tower?" Porkchop asked as I emerged from the tent.

"Yes!" I said eagerly. You don't get that offer very often, and I was curious to see what things were like behind the scenes.

The afternoon airshow had begun, so everyone from the tower was hanging out in their break room—including the controller who had given me the go around and then landed me.

"Just so you know," I said, relieved to get to actually talk back now that we weren't on the radio, "I was going to hit that green dot like my life depended on it!"

He chuckled. "Well, you never know."

"I can't believe that pilot behind me who requested a

touch-and-go," I said. This had been bugging me since my landing: A guy two planes back had asked for permission to do a touch-and-go, which meant that he just wanted to touch down on the runway and then take off again, clearly something he only wanted to do so that he could say that he'd landed at Oshkosh and record it in his logbook. And that's fine when things are slow ... but with the high volume of traffic coming through, it was an absolutely absurd and selfish request.

"Look," my new controller friend had said to him, "you may be new here, but in my nineteen years here, this is the first touch-and-go I've ever heard of!" But then he let him do it!

The controller shrugged. "It was annoying. But not such a big deal."

"If I were you," I said, "I would have told him to get the hell out of the airspace!"

He laughed. "Next time." He clearly had a lot more patience than I did.

After spending a little more time chatting in the break room, Porkchop took us upstairs to the tower cab and we got to talk to the woman in charge of the controllers.

"I don't know how you guys do it," I said, shaking my head. "It's mayhem out there!"

"It's actually not as crazy as it was last year," she said. "Traffic is down one thousand landings versus this time last year."

Hard to tell from my perspective!

There were colored dots taped to the windows to correspond with the colored dots on the runway so the tower controllers could quickly spot them. The tower cab also offered a priceless view of the thousands of planes parked everywhere on the field below. And it was air-conditioned—a rare treat in that heat!

After dinner at a local joint, it was time for a shower and some much-needed catch-up sleep. But it was still, like, a *trillion* degrees out, and we were sweating like pigs. As nice as a shower would feel, we agreed that we were too tired to deal with walking to the showers, changing while still sweaty from the shower steam-room heat and humidity, and walking back. So we both stripped down as much as we could, I opened both air flaps to the tent—I didn't really care if some stranger walked by and saw me in my undies and bra, it was that hot—and we lay down on top of our sleeping bags to try to get some shut-eye.

I was now regretting that I had not taken my father's suggestion and bought an air mattress to cushion the unforgiving hardness of the ground. I'd figured that 1) it would be grassy on the field and therefore relatively soft, and 2) I was in no position, in my unemployed state, to purchase something I'd use only once. *Hindsight*, I thought as a rock dug into my back. I could feel my muscles seizing up as I lay there sweating. I tried to shift my sleeping bag around to avoid the hard spot, but in this sliver of a "four-person" tent, there wasn't much room for maneuvering. It was either lie on my back and shove my spine up towards my ribcage, or lie on my stomach and squish my boobs into my shoulder blades. I had also developed a personal pool of sweat that I was now simmering in. *Ugh.*

I was feeling very stupid for having conveniently forgotten how much I hate camping. I seriously thought that because Airventure was all about planes, that would somehow magically make this part enjoyable. Unfortunately, as I was now finding out the hard way—pun intended—as cool as airplanes are, they don't make the ground any softer.

Joelle seemed to be nodding off, but I could tell she was pretty uncomfortable, too, since she was tossing a lot. Still, we were both so exhausted. Even I was on the verge of sleep—and then that storm that we had beat there arrived, loudly and brightly announcing its arrival. Lightning began to flash every few seconds. *Oh boy.*

Joelle rolled over and looked at me, droopy-eyed. I groaned. *Can this possibly get any worse?* Then some obviously terrified kid a few tents over started screaming bloody murder. *Apparently it can.*

"Jesus," Joelle said. "It sounds like his parents are trying to cut his finger off or something!"

It just went on and on. Every time I thought he'd run out of breath or screamed his throat raw, he took a breath and kept wailing. I shoved my earplugs into my ear canals as far as they could go, and it still sounded as if he were in our tent. And the lightning continued.

Again I was close to passing out—despite the lightning, and despite the kid attempting to be heard in China—but then it started to rain. And if you don't know this, let me tell you: Rain is mighty loud inside a tent. I guess it had never rained on my previous two camping trips.

It was one of those what-else-could-possibly-go-wrong moments, so much so that Joelle and I looked at each other and both burst out laughing.

This isn't even funny! I thought. *This SUCKS!* But I kept laughing. And it kept raining.

I accepted defeat. I whipped out my phone and started checking e-mails. We had only gotten to charge our phones for a few minutes at the shower facility—the only place in the camping area where there was electricity—so my battery life was running low. I guess this lack of outlet options would come as no surprise to people who camp, but it was a rude awakening for me. What do you mean I can't charge up my phone, laptop, GPS receiver, iPad, digital camera, and digital video camera while I sleep? I had more charging cords than you could shake a stick at, and nothing to do with them.

As if the rain, lightning, and screaming child weren't enough, the tent began to leak. In multiple places. I moved my suitcase and clothes away from the leaks and, shielding my phone from rogue drops of water, wrote an e-mail to my dad, who had warned me that I wasn't the camping type. The subject line was "Hello Muddah, Hello Fadduh," after the old song. The e-mail itself was an endless rant about how much camping did indeed suck. Writing it was cathartic for me, and I knew my father would get a kick out of it. I looked forward to his "I told you so" response e-mail.

As I wrapped up my e-mail, it occurred to me that Porkchop had mentioned during dinner that he had two beds in his hotel room, and offered one to us in case the whole camping thing didn't work out. Why is it that my friends often know me better than I know myself? At the time, I'd thought it was an overly kind gesture—something I would never take him up on. I didn't want to impose. Now I couldn't wait for morning to come so I could do just that.

The rain finally stopped coming down at some point, but the wind kept blowing, and with every gust of wind, cold water showered down on us from where it was leaking into the tent. There was still lightning in the distance, too, and every flash lit up my world, even with my eyes closed. The kid, at least, had finally either fallen asleep or been killed by a neighboring camper.

I looked over at Joelle: asleep. How, I didn't know. I rose and walked around outside in the dark for a little while, bored and lacking anything else to do. I crawled back into the tent a little before 4:00 a.m., and finally—*finally*—managed to doze off for a while.

Then 6:00 a.m. hit, and the airport opened up again. Planes

were taking off about every thirty seconds. I was so tired that I was able to sleep off and on, between the departures, for a couple of hours. But after a couple of hours of that, it was too much. I gave up.

EXHAUSTED BUT STILL FEELING LUCKY TO BE AT Airventure, Joelle and I decided to make the best of our day. We walked around the airport, enjoying the airplanes on display. I guarantee that if something has flown, has tried to fly, or has hopes to fly in the future, some version of it will be at Oshkosh. You overhear a lot of "Wow, I didn't know that still existed!" and "I haven't seen one of those in fifty years" there. You see the latest attempt at a flying car, World War II bombers and dogfighters, planes from even before WWII, military jets and helicopters, blimps, gliders, all manner of taildraggers, fancy aerobatic planes with all their sponsor logos all over them, and thousands of airplanes similar to mine. It truly is an airplane lover's heaven—every time you turn your head, there's some amazing aircraft that quite possibly can only be seen once a year, there at Oshkosh.

We took our chairs across the field to the grass runway for the "ultralights" (gliders, helicopters, autogyros), where we sat down to watch a three-hour-long helicopter airshow. About twenty minutes into the show, it started to rain. And normally rain is no big deal—but it was pouring, and I had my laptop in my backpack. We ran into a large tent nearby, along with everyone else who had been watching the helicopter show, and waited it out.

The downpour only lasted about ten minutes, but with the threat of more rain on the way, the helicopter show was cancelled. We walked in a light drizzle to meet Porkchop, who had just finished his shift.

I didn't wait long to ask the question that was pressing on my mind: "Does that offer to stay on the extra bed in your room still stand?"

"Of course!" Porkchop said.

Joelle and I exchanged a look of relief. "Thank god!"

"Why don't you take my car so we don't have to carry your luggage from the tent to the hotel?" he said. "I can catch a ride there with another controller later."

What a guy.

Just as Porkchop was handing me his car keys, the skies opened up yet again. Having lived in New Orleans for most of my life, it takes a helluva hard rain to catch my attention. This one did. We ran under another large tent, but the wind was blowing so hard that even on the far leeward side of the tent, we were getting soaked. I spotted a few people running through an open door into a nearby building.

I elbowed Joelle. "What do you think is in there?"

She shrugged. "I don't know, but it has to be better than this!"

We ran for it.

The "room" turned out to be a storage closet—but it was a *dry* storage closet. Joelle and I happily jammed into it with the four strangers already inside.

Once again, the rain only lasted about ten minutes, but it was one of the hardest rains I'd ever seen. I hoped my plane was okay.

Just as things were letting up, another couple seeking shelter ran past.

"Come on in!" I said, beckoning them over.

They glanced inside. "Looks a little crowded!" the woman said. She glanced up at the sky. "It seems to be calming down anyway. Did you guys hear about the biplane that flipped over?"

We collectively shook our heads.

"A homebuilt biplane broke its tiedowns during the storm and flipped over onto another airplane."

"Was anyone hurt?" Joelle asked.

"No," the woman said, "but the planes are pretty wrecked."

Shit. Now I really started to worry about my plane and how it had fared in the wind.

Joelle and I braved the drizzle and briskly walked the fifteen minutes back to my plane to check on it. From a distance, we could see that the plane was fine and still tied down. What a relief!

The tent, however, was flattened. Decimated. As we drew closer to the tent, I saw that the only thing keeping it from not looking entirely like a pancake was our now-drowned luggage. The wind had broken one of the poles. We tried to stick the pieces back together, but there was no way they were going to stay. If I were in the cavalry, I would have shot the poor thing to put it out of its misery.

Well, that settled it: the tent was now uninhabitable. Not that I was second-guessing moving into my friend's cozy hotel room. I'd have to share a double bed with another woman, but compared to the hard, wet ground, with its surround-sound, guaranteed-to-keep-you-awake cacophony, that setup sounded downright luxurious.

I got inside the tent so I could hold it up and assess the situation inside. I picked up Joelle's suitcase to pass it to her outside the tent ... and it gushed water. Ditto with my suitcase. So now we had not a single piece of dry clothing between us. Meanwhile, our sleeping bags weighed about fifty pounds apiece; it took both of us to drag them out and hang them on the struts of the airplane—to dry, we hoped.

A gentleman from somewhere in the North 40 was going tent to tent with a gallon jug that he'd cut the top off of to turn it into a scoop. "Do you need your tent bailed out?" he asked when he got to us, very nonchalant.

Are we the only ones who didn't get the memo that this kind of torrential downpour is normal? I wondered.

He saw how badly our tent was flooded. "Here, let me—"

"Don't bother," I said, holding a hand up to stop him. "This tent is definitely DNR!"

Just then, my phone buzzed. Porkchop, texting to tell us there was a dryer in his hotel. I showed Joelle. "Does he have ESP or what?" I said incredulously, shaking my head.

We thanked the generous stranger with the makeshift scoop for his attempted rescue, and went to find Porkchop's car —and then, after finding the hotel, spent the rest of the day drying our clothes rather than looking at the airplanes we had flown seven and a half hours to see.

It took two dryer cycles in an industrial dryer to totally dry our thoroughly soaked wardrobes. I sat there on the folding counter in the hotel laundry room, tired, a little dazed, and still soaked since we couldn't strip naked to dry the clothes we had on, and rewrote the lyrics to "Hello Muddah, Hello Fadduh" in my head to pass the time:

Hello muddah, hello fadduh,
Here I am at Camp North 40
Oshkosh is very entertaining
And we had a tent until it started raining.

I thought it was pretty funny, anyway.

THE NEXT DAY, PORKCHOP DROPPED US OFF AT THE airport and we went to check on the state of affairs of our "campsite." It had rained again during the night, but it must not have been a windy rain, because our sleeping bags, thanks to the shelter of Orion's wings, were now dry. The tent, however, had breathed its last breath: it had now completely flattened under the weight of the rain. I didn't want to put it into the airplane wet, so we unstaked it and hung various parts of it around the airplane to dry.

After a couple hours in the sun and wind, the tent pieces were *mostly* dry—good enough for us, anyway—so we threw everything in the plane and headed out to the flight line to enjoy the afternoon airshow.

It was a veritable smorgasbord of aircraft: Zeros, Pitts, Extras, Mustangs, Stearmans, AWACS, the Red Bull aerobatic helicopter, the Goodyear blimp, and all manner of fighter jets doing tons of fun things that made me completely jealous. They set off pyrotechnics on the far side of the runway to re-enact *Tora! Tora! Tora!*, with airplanes buzzing in every direction in mock bombing runs. Fire, things blowing up, loud airplanes zooming in every direction—it truly was aviation heaven! I planted my lawn chair on the flightline and—for the first time since we got there—relaxed and enjoyed the show.

By this time it was Friday—almost time to go home. So that afternoon, we went to get a weather briefing from the Flight Service tent near the North 40. Just as had happened the day prior, we were standing in line, waiting our turn, when a man cut in front of us. The first time, we just looked at each other and rolled our eyes. The second time, I guess the guy saw us do that and realized what he'd done: "Oh, were you two here for a briefing? I thought you were with that guy," he said as he pointed to a man near us.

When we approached the briefer, he started and said basically the same thing as the other guy: "Oh, I'm sorry, you were waiting? I thought you ladies were with that guy."

Of course. It never ceases to amaze me how difficult it is for male aviators to understand that women fly too.

The briefer told us that the weather was probably going to get worse Saturday afternoon, so we decided to head out Saturday morning, hopefully avoiding the summer afternoon thunderstorms around New Orleans by arriving in the early evening. It felt like we'd just gotten to Oshkosh, and it was already time to go.

FRUSTRATING AS IT OFTEN IS THAT THE FLYING WORLD IS so male-centric, as I've said before, being a woman pilot comes with some advantages. When Joelle and I started making preparations to leave on Saturday morning, we found that my plane had sunk a bit into the wet ground—there was no way just the two of us could push it out into the open, where we could start it without blasting anyone behind us. I spotted a group of four men who were chatting a few planes over. Bingo.

"My plane's a bit stuck," I said, sidling over. "Think you guys would be willing to help us push it out?"

"Of course!" they said, hurrying over. Problem solved.

As we made our way back to the runway, I began to wonder where, if anywhere, I could do my pre-takeoff checks. I couldn't see anyone in the line of airplanes taxiing in front of me stopping to do it. *Am I missing something?* I wondered.

Just as I touched the taxiway leading up to the runway, I heard "White and red Cessna, clear for takeoff" on the tower frequency.

I looked around for another red and white Cessna. "Do you think that was for us?" I asked Joelle.

Then it came again: "White and red Cessna, clear for takeoff."

"I guess that's us!" Joelle said.

So much for doing the pre-takeoff checks! I gunned it and said goodbye to my beloved green dot on runway 27. They were launching planes off about every thirty seconds, so I had to keep my eyes peeled for slower traffic in front of me and faster traffic behind me, but we made it out without incident.

Joelle and I were both sad to leave Airventure—especially since we'd spent so little time there actually enjoying the sights —but we were both looking forward to sleeping in our own beds that night. When your only options are the wet ground or a shared hotel bed for a few nights, you really start to appreciate the small things.

As I flew back while Joelle napped next to me, I reflected upon my journey—not just to Oshkosh, but as a pilot. I had started flying when I was twenty-three, bought a plane when I was twenty-four, and now, at thirty-two, I was a much more confident, purposeful person, and had amassed a wonderful and eclectic group of friends all over the US and around the world—due in no small part to aviation. In many ways, I had grown up in the very plane I was currently piloting.

I thought what I was like when I first started flying—unsure of what to do with my life, dating a guy I should have dumped the second he said his first chauvinistic comment, unaware that I could have just as much control over my life as I did over an airplane if I just took the initiative—and smiled to realize just how far I had come. I knew what I was doing with my life. I'd learned what was acceptable behavior and what wasn't in a romantic partner. I had a job that allowed me to use my plane as often as I wanted. And I had even made it to Mecca.

I hope that the stars will align again soon so I can go back to Oshkosh and see all that I missed the first time around. But I think next time I'll skip the camping.

 *Epilogue* |

POSTCARDS
FROM THE SKY

Do not follow where the path may lead.
Go instead where there is no path and leave a trail.
—RALPH WALDO EMERSON

BEFORE WRITING THIS BOOK, I'D TOLD THE STORY of my first flying lesson and Bill's "there goes another empty kitchen" comment dozens of times—sometimes to an audience of all men at the airport, sometimes to girl-friends who aren't pilots, and sometimes to a (small) audience of women at the airport who are involved in aviation in some way or another, whether as pilots, instructors, or employees at the local FBO. I'm sure you can imagine the many reactions I've had to that story. Some of the men snicker, perhaps seeing themselves as thinking or even saying something like that. Some are just downright appalled—which, of course, is the reaction *I* think everyone, male and female, should have to that statement.

My favorite responses, however, are those that offer great zingers that we only think of long after a conversation is over—you know, the kind that make you wish you could time travel back and fling one at the other party as a riposte. I'd love to go back and get to use one of those zingers on Bill—although, come to think of it, if I could really go back in time maybe I'd just take back having dated Bill for two years.

Despite my regrets, however, I can say that my relationship with Bill taught me what traits I will and will not accept in a man—like chauvinism, for example—and it's a lesson I'm grateful for. And ignoring Bill's contribution, flying in general has taught me many ways to turn something negative into something positive. Some men say a lot of terrible things to female pilots, and though I always feel an initial shock when I hear them, ultimately they have the exact opposite of their intended effect because they inspire me to prove them wrong—and to be a model pilot to anyone thinking of getting into aviation, male or female.

I MET THE LAST SURVIVING TUSKEEGEE AIRMAN FROM Louisiana over Mardi Gras recently when he rode as a guest in the same parade I ride in, the Krewe of Orpheus.

I introduced myself and shook his hand. "I know what it's like to be a minority in aviation," I said.

"Well, ya'll were in the air long before us!" he responded.

And it was true, of course. In many ways, especially when it comes to inclusivity and diversity, aviation has a long way to go. But as an unlikely traveler who later turned into an unlikely pilot, I now cannot imagine my life without the world of aviation—flawed as it is—being a huge part of it. And if you can look past the guys who have horrible put-downs for women pilots, there are so many more exceptionally friendly, generous, and caring souls involved in aviation who make me so happy to be part of their group. It's a passion that continues to grow for me each day. And even though flights in my small plane are more sensitive to changes in weather and winds, those very changes and uncertainties are what keep the excitement and mystery alive—what keep this airsickness-prone, camping-averse traveler always daydreaming of the next flight, where it will take me, and the lifelong memories that it will create.

The most incredible part is, these wonderful and spontaneous adventures are available to anyone, man or woman, who is willing to learn the art of flying. If you even have the slightest interest in aviation, I encourage you to drive straight to your local airport, whether it's a big commercial air service airport or a smaller airport that only serves general aviation, and talk to people. You will likely find a friendly pilot willing to take you up for a ride. And that ride may just change your life.

When I was going for my commercial rating, my instructor said something that really struck a chord with me: "When you're in the cockpit, you aren't a man or a woman. You're a pilot."

I've also heard people say, "Who cares what gender you are? The airplane certainly doesn't know!"

Clearly the rest of the world doesn't always see things this way—and not just in aviation. But I don't let it get to me. I have my plane, and I always have my next adventure on the horizon. And that's enough for me.

ACKNOWLEDGMENTS

First, to everyone who listened to my stories and laughed or cried (sometimes both) and then said, "You know, you really should write a book," enough of you said it that I finally did. Then, once it was written, thanks to Brian for reading my first draft and not saying it was terrible. Brooke Warner, the editing staff at Warner Coaching, and everyone at She Writes Press, thank you for everything you did to get my thoughts into print. As an editor myself, I never look forward to working with a new editor. Will she "get" me? Will she try to put words in my mouth? Krissa Lagos did both with total grace, and the words she put in my mouth were the ones I couldn't quite figure out how to say myself. Thank you.

To all my flying buddies past and present and scattered all over the four corners of the world, thank you now and always for inspiration, encouragement, and camaraderie.

Finally and most passionately, thank you to my family and especially my parents. Throughout my life of odd hobby choices (fencing, then bagpiping, then flying, a few not so noteworthy ones in between, and who knows what's next?), even if they thought it was ridiculous or that I'd never stick with it, they supported me nonetheless. As long as it made me happy, they were happy. I hope I have made you equally happy in return.

About the Author

ERIN SEIDEMANN was born and raised in New Orleans in Southeastern Louisiana, a part of the state often described as "south of the South." She attended Loyola University New Orleans and graduated cum laude with a degree in English writing. She recently earned her commercial pilot license and bought a twin-engine plane so she can explore even more of the world. You can find more of her writing at www.agirlandherplane.com.

SELECTED TITLES FROM SHE WRITES PRESS

Peanut Butter and Naan: Stories of an American Mother in The Far East by Jennifer Magnuson. $16.95, 978-1-63152-911-5. The hilarious tale of what happened when Jennifer Magnuson moved her family of seven from Nashville to India in an effort to shake things up—and got more than she bargained for.

This is Mexico: Tales of Culture and Other Complications by Carol M. Merchasin. $16.95, 978-1-63152-962-7. Merchasin chronicles her attempts to understand Mexico, her adopted country, through improbable situations and small moments that keep the reader moving between laughter and tears.

Flip-Flops After Fifty: And Other Thoughts on Aging I Remembered to Write Down by Cindy Eastman. $16.95, 978-1-938314-68-1. A collection of frank and funny essays about turning fifty—and all the emotional ups and downs that come with it.

Daring to Date Again: A Memoir by Ann Anderson Evans. $16.95, 978-1-63152-909-2. A hilarious, no-holds-barred memoir about a legal secretary turned professor who dives back into the dating pool headfirst after twelve years of celibacy.

Insatiable: A Memoir of Love Addiction by Shary Hauer. $16.95, 978-1-63152-982-5. An intimate and illuminating account of corporate executive—and secret love addict—Shary Hauer's migration from destructive to healthy love.

Renewable: One Woman's Search for Simplicity, Faithfulness, and Hope by Eileen Flanagan. $16.95, 978-1-63152-968-9. At age forty-nine, Eileen Flanagan had an aching feeling that she wasn't living up to her youthful ideals or potential, so she started trying to change the world—and in doing so, she found the courage to change her life.